HOME REPAIR AND IMPROVEMENT

HOME OFFICES

TIME®
LIFE
BOOKS

OTHER PUBLICATIONS:

DO IT YOURSELF
The Time-Life Complete Gardener
Home Repair and Improvement
The Art of Woodworking
Fix It Yourself

COOKING
Weight Watchers® Smart Choice Recipe Collection
Great Taste/Low Fat
Williams-Sonoma Kitchen Library

HISTORY
The American Story
Voices of the Civil War
The American Indians
Lost Civilizations
Mysteries of the Unknown
Time Frame
The Civil War
Cultural Atlas

TIME-LIFE KIDS
Library of First Questions and Answers
A Child's First Library of Learning
I Love Math
Nature Company Discoveries
Understanding Science & Nature

SCIENCE/NATURE
Voyage Through the Universe

For information on and a full description
of any of the Time-Life Books series listed above,
please call 1-800-621-7026 or write:

Reader Information
Time-Life Customer Service
P.O. Box C-32068
Richmond Virginia 23261-2068

HOME REPAIR AND IMPROVEMENT

HOME OFFICES

BY THE EDITORS OF TIME-LIFE BOOKS, ALEXANDRIA, VIRGINIA

The Consultants

L. T. Bowden, Jr. has been a master electrician and electrical contractor for 18 years, working in commercial, residential, and industrial electrical contracting, as well as specializing in residential electrical service work. He has been an electrical apprenticeship instructor for the past eight years, and is currently General Manager of D & K Electric Inc., a contracting firm in northern Virginia.

Jon Eakes is a renovation expert known for his television series *Renovation Zone* and his home improvement call-in television show, *Just Ask*. He also works in other media, including radio and print, and has his own home video series. Mr. Eakes teaches construction courses to contractors and is an active member of the Technical Research Committee of the Canadian Home Builder's Association. He heads Interface Productions, an advertising and marketing company dealing with the renovation sector.

Sheryl Johnston is an interior designer with 20 years of experience working in commercial and residential design. She started her own company, Design Essentials, in Montreal in 1993, specializing in both ergonomic custom design and home office design.

François St-Pierre is a cabinetmaker in Lac-Mégantic, Quebec, with 20 years of woodworking experience, primarily in custom-built office furniture. In addition, he has worked in the construction industry, and designs and builds theater sets and circus equipment.

Joe Teets is a master electrician/contractor. Currently in the Office of Adult and Community Education for the Fairfax County Public Schools, he has been involved in apprenticeship training as an instructor and coordinator since 1985.

CONTENTS

Planning Your Home Office

Millions of Americans have found a way to bypass morning traffic jams. For them, the morning commute is nothing more than a short walk across the hall or down the stairs—or out the back door to what was once the garage. The first step in realizing your dream of a new home office is to find the space for it. Then you're ready to draw up a plan for an office tailored to meet your needs.

An office tucked into a closet →

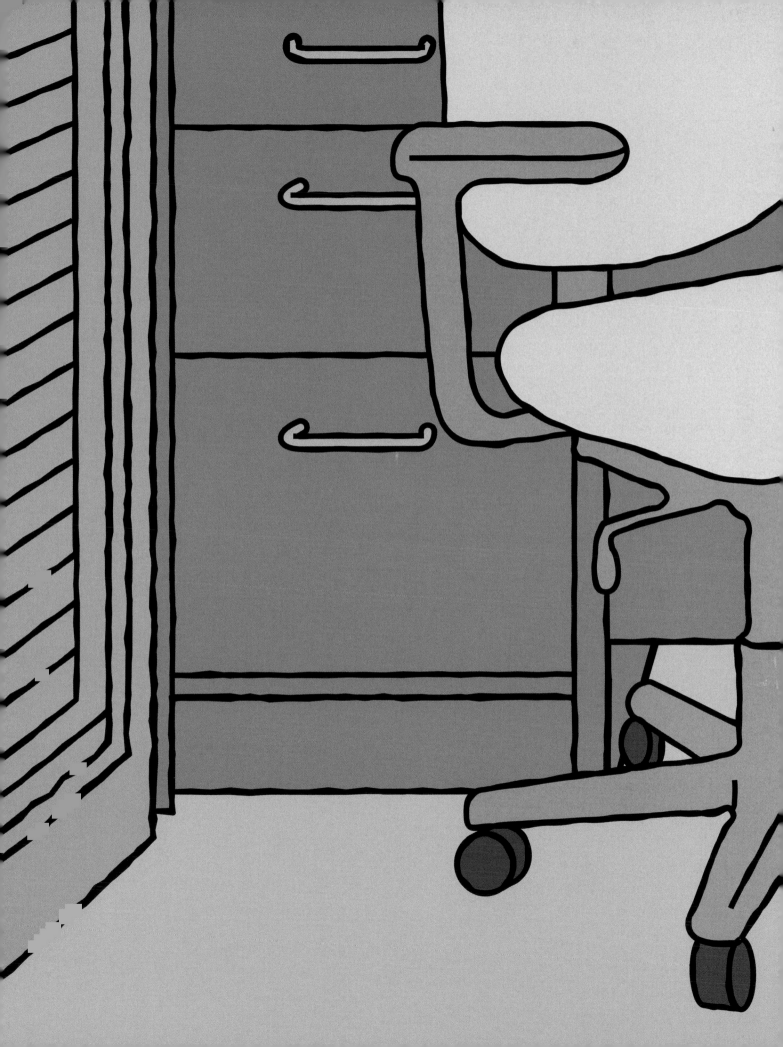

Finding the Space

Often, the biggest stumbling block to setting up a home office is finding the space. If you already have a spare room in your house, that may be the most obvious solution. If not, you will need to either adapt an existing room to accommodate the office, or create a new room by converting an unfinished space. Before making a choice, take the time to determine your space requirements carefully. In choosing between possible locations, you may want to develop a detailed floor plan for each *(pages 12-17)*. Other considerations—how separate from the rest of the house the space feels, for example—are equally important *(below)*.

Adapting an Existing Room: Almost any room in the house can serve double duty as an office. However, locating an office in a living room or bedroom, for example, can create a conflict between your need for a private working area and the activities of family members. In addition, setting up the office in a corner of an existing room may not provide enough psychological separation between your working and living spaces. A simple solution is to define the area visually. You can build a screen divider *(pages 26-27)* or buy a commercial one. If the room is large enough, building a permanent wall between the working and living areas may be more satisfactory *(pages 20-25)*.

Hidden Space: An examination of your home may yield some surprises. A small office can often be tucked into an unused corner such as the space under a stairway, or perhaps you can free a large closet *(page 11)*.

Creating a New Space: Converting an unfinished attic, basement, or garage *(opposite and page 10)* is generally a more expensive option than adapting an existing room. However, such a renovation may be the best way to gain privacy for your office. Creating a new room also allows you to tailor the space to meet your needs. If your budget allows, building an addition may be the best way to create the ideal office space.

Choosing a Space

Any space in your house will likely require at least minor renovations in order to meet all the requirements listed below. However, the following points will help you choose a space that can be transformed into a satisfactory working area with the least trouble and expense.

✔ Is your space large enough to accommodate all office activities? Is there storage space at hand?

✔ Is the area adequately isolated from noise and odors from elsewhere in the house? Will the sound of office equipment be bothersome to other family members?

✔ Does the space feel psychologically separate from the rest of the house? Is it a space where you feel both alert and relaxed?

✔ If you expect visitors, will they have to walk through or past private areas of the house to reach the office? Would it be possible to install a separate entrance?

✔ Does the room have sufficient electrical outlets and phone jacks for an office? Will you need to add new electrical circuits?

✔ Is there adequate lighting? Are there windows?

✔ Is the space well ventilated, heated, and cooled? Is it dry?

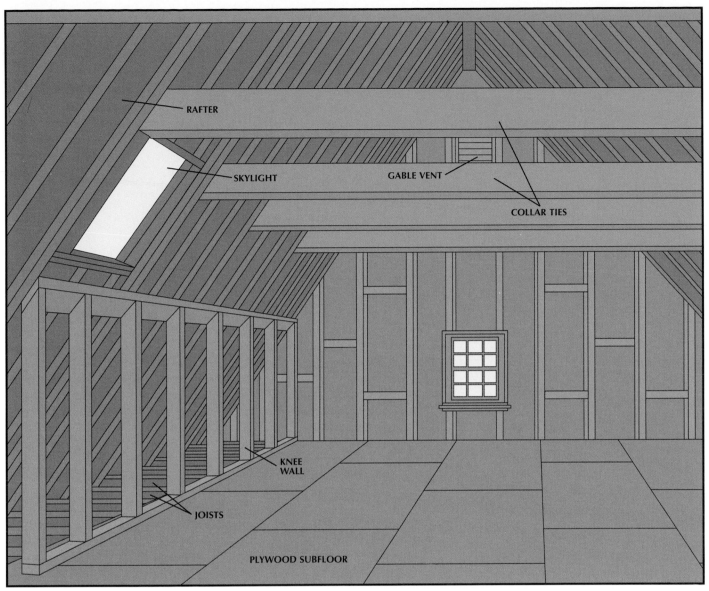

RAFTER

SKYLIGHT

GABLE VENT

COLLAR TIES

KNEE WALL

JOISTS

PLYWOOD SUBFLOOR

Converting an attic.

An unfinished attic can be transformed into an attractive and spacious work area, but a number of adaptations are necessary. Before installing a floor, check whether the floor joists can adequately bear the load of people and furniture. Joists made from 2-by-6s on 16-inch centers can span up to 8 feet, while 2-by-8 joists can span 11 feet. If the joists exceed these spans, double them by fastening a second joist to each. You may want to add insulation between joists for its soundproofing qualities before installing a plywood subfloor over the joists to support the new flooring materials.

The sloping walls of the attic can be a problem for placing furniture. To square off the walls, install short partitions called knee walls running from the floor to the rafters. About 5 feet is a convenient height. In some cases, knee walls are required by code.

To make the ceiling easier to insulate, square it off with collar ties, attaching one tie to each pair of rafters. *(In the illustration above, some collar ties have been removed for clarity.)* A good ceiling height is $7\frac{1}{2}$ feet. Make sure the area above the new ceiling is adequately ventilated, with a gable vent or fan. If there is inadequate headroom in the attic, consider building in a gable dormer. A skylight is another attractive addition.

Insulate the attic knee walls, the ceiling, the floor area behind the knee walls, and the exposed rafters with fiberglass batts so the vapor barrier faces toward the room. When insulating rafters, create a 1-inch gap between the insulation and the roof sheathing with cardboard baffles. Between floor joists, do not jam the insulation against the eaves—this will block the airflow. After the insulation is in place, finish the walls and ceiling with wallboard.

Provide access to your attic office with a stairway at least 36 inches wide, with steps no less than $8\frac{1}{4}$ inches high and 9 inches deep.

The simplest way to heat the attic office is to install heating registers to allow warm air to rise from below, but cold winters may call for electric baseboard heaters.

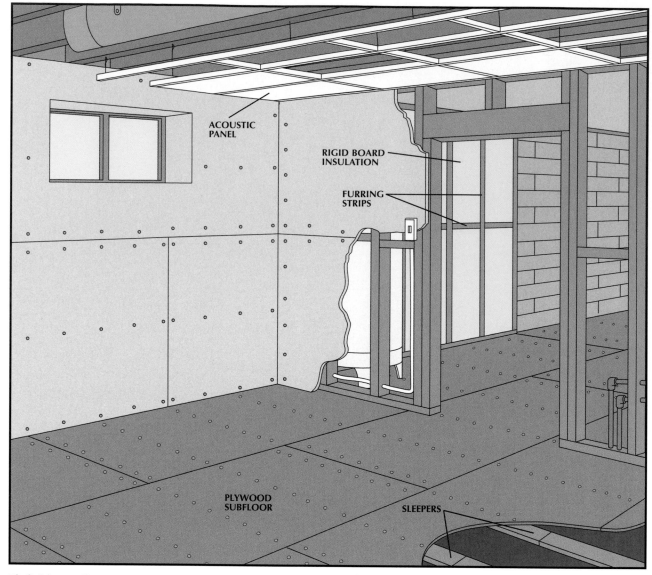

ACOUSTIC
PANEL

RIGID BOARD
INSULATION

FURRING
STRIPS

PLYWOOD
SUBFLOOR

SLEEPERS

Finishing a basement.

To make a basement habitable, first correct any moisture problem. Seepage from outside usually can be prevented by roof gutters and downspouts, soil grading, and proper drainage to direct water away from the foundation. Condensation from inside can be controlled by using a dehumidifier, venting clothes dryers to the outside, and wrapping water pipes with insulation.

As underpinnings for a floor, first lay down building paper, then fasten pressure-treated-wood sleepers to the concrete. In cold climates, you can insulate the floor with rigid foam boards laid between the sleepers. Extruded polystyrene foam is best,

requiring no vapor barrier. Nail a plywood subfloor to the sleepers.

To finish masonry walls, construct a stud wall insulated with fiberglass batts. Or, you can add polystyrene boards, securing them with furring strips nailed to the wall through the insulation.

If you decide to wall off basement appliances such as a furnace or water heater, leave 3 feet of space around the equipment and provide for adequate ventilation.

Many building codes require 7 feet, 6 inches of headroom for a finished room. If you're short on space, you can leave the ceiling unfinished and

paint everything overhead—including pipes and ducts—a light color.

A wallboard ceiling takes little room and can be installed on resilient channels to absorb noise from above *(page 40)*. However, you will have to reroute or raise ducts and pipes that extend below joists. If you can spare the headroom, a suspended ceiling *(above)* can be built below ducts and pipes, while leaving them easily accessible *(page 37)*.

You can heat a finished basement by tapping into a forced-air heating system. Or you can install baseboard heaters to provide an independent heat source.

UNCOVERING HIDDEN SPACE

An office in a closet.

If you're really pressed for space, a large closet can accommodate a small office—20 inches deep is a bare minimum. If you don't have enough room to fit a standard desk *(right)*, you can support a work surface with cleats on the closet walls, and install shelves for storage *(pages 118-121)*. If the doorway is too small to make the space accessible, consider widening the opening and adding bifold doors.

If your office will house electronic equipment that must run continuously, ventilation may be inadequate when the doors are closed. Louvered doors, or a vent into the next room, are two possible solutions.

Under the stairs.

The unused space under a stairway may be just enough for a small work space. Shelves can be attached to the wall under the stairs. To blend the work area into its surroundings, finish the desk and shelving to match the stairway. To save on space, you can attach a lamp to the back wall, or to the back of a stair riser.

11

Drawing Up a Plan

Designing sample floor plans of your proposed new office will help you choose and arrange office furniture, and will also serve as a guide for the renovations required to adapt the space to your needs. Specialized computer programs are available to help you develop a floor plan, but you can also draw your own.

Base Map: Draw a base map such as the one below so you have a detailed scale plan of your existing space. A workable scale is $\frac{1}{2}$ inch to 1 foot. Use graph paper with $\frac{1}{4}$-inch squares.

Adding Furniture: The next step is to determine the dimensions of the furniture and equipment you will need. To sketch potential layouts, make a number of copies of the base map and draw in the furniture, or design each layout on a piece of tracing paper placed over the base map. Alternatively, draw scale silhouettes of your proposed furniture and equipment, cut them out, and arrange them on the base map (self-adhesive notepaper works well for this). Several examples of home-office layouts are illustrated on pages 14 to 17.

Don't stop at a desk and chair—try to anticipate other furniture that your activities will require, such as a stand for a photocopier, a conference table, a second desk for a co-worker, or a large cutting table for a sewing business. Be sure to leave adequate maneuvering room around each piece of furniture (*opposite*).

Refining the Plan: As you arrange the furniture, note any changes you would like to make to the space. You may want to add dividers or walls to separate different work activities (*pages 20-27*); you may even consider removing a wall to create a more open area (*pages 28-30*). Once the sketch is finished, you will also be able to plan any modifications needed to the lighting and wiring (*Chapter 3*).

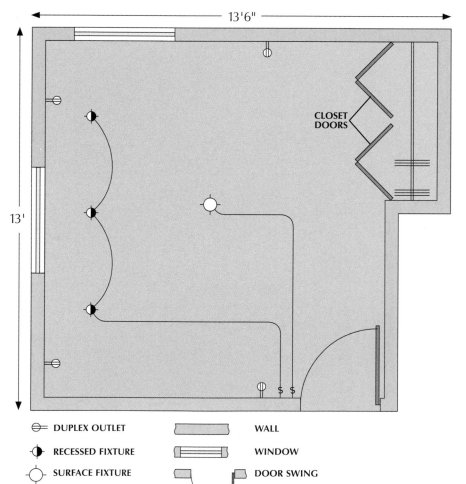

⊖	DUPLEX OUTLET	▭	WALL
◖	RECESSED FIXTURE	▭	WINDOW
○	SURFACE FIXTURE	⌐	DOOR SWING
$	SINGLE SWITCH		

CLOSET DOORS

13'6"

13'

Preparing a base map.

First, carefully measure your space. After determining the overall dimensions of the room, draw the perimeter of the room to scale. Then, determine the size and location of any openings such as windows, doors, and closets, and add them to the drawing. (You might also want to record the height of the windows to help with the placement of cabinets.) Note which direction each door opens and, with a compass, draw in an arc representing the space taken up by the swing of the door. Finally, add to your plan locations of any existing electrical features such as switches, outlets, and lighting fixtures. Standard symbols used by designers for these elements are shown in the legend below.

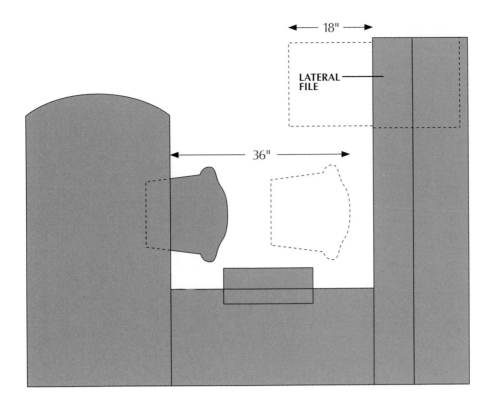

LATERAL FILE

18"

36"

Space requirements.

As you arrange furniture on your base map, be sure to leave enough room for chairs and open file cabinets. For example, allow at least 36 inches for a chair to be pushed away from a desk *(left, top)*. Measure this distance from the edge of the desk to the back of the chair when it is pulled out. Lateral files require 18 inches to open fully. If you are setting up a conference area *(left, bottom)*, allow 36 inches behind each chair and 32 inches between chair centers for elbow room.

36"

32"

CONFERENCE TABLE

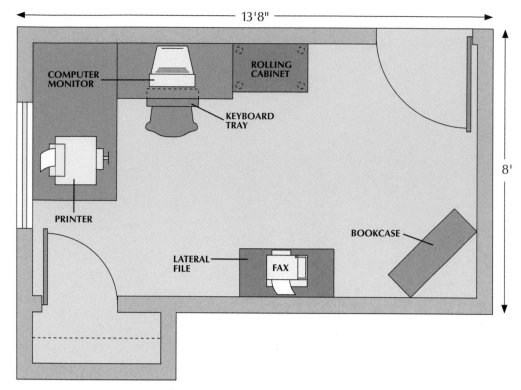

A small office.

An L-shaped computer workstation makes the best use of space in this small one-person office. Next to the desk stands a rolling cabinet that can be pulled around to serve as an additional work surface. A fax machine sits on a lateral file, and a bookcase spans the corner.

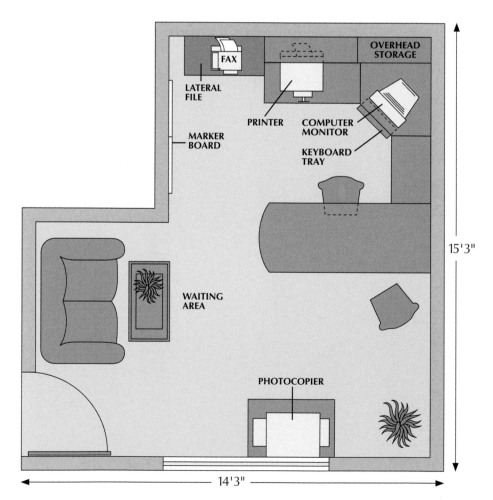

A medium-size office.

This one-person office features a generous U-shaped workstation with ample desk space for a computer monitor, a printer, and paperwork, as well as overhead storage. A marker board—for erasable felt pens—is hung on the wall behind the workstation. The space on top of the lateral file is occupied by a fax machine, while a separate table houses a photocopier. To accommodate visitors, an extra chair can be pulled up to one wing of the desk or, for less formal meetings, moved toward the coffee table in a waiting area set up near the office entrance.

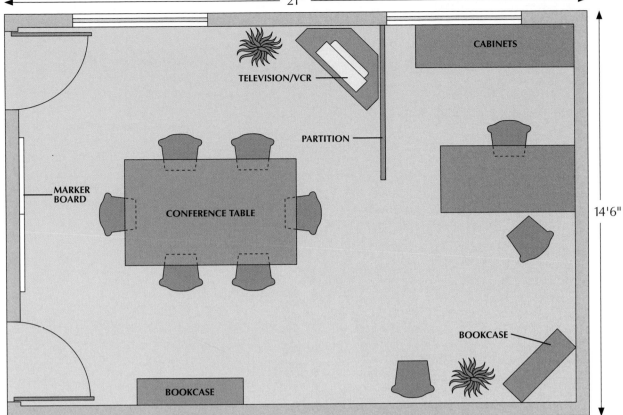

Office with a conference area.

If your business involves meetings and you have sufficient space to host them, consider including a conference area in your office plan. This one has a corner unit with a television for video presentations. One wall is devoted to a white marker board. The work area is screened by a partition—a commercial screen would do the job, or a half-height wall could be built. Additional chairs accommodate one-on-one meetings, and low cabinets along one wall store promotional or reference materials. A laptop computer is stowed away when not in use.

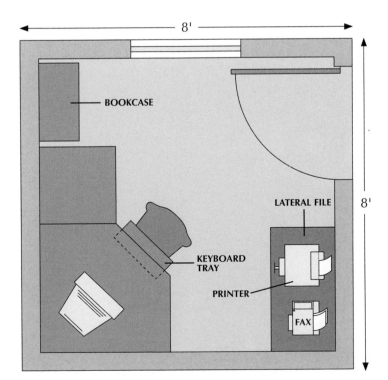

An alcove office.

A functional office can fit into even a small area like this one. Locating the computer workstation in a corner saves on space. There is even room for a small bookcase and a lateral file with enough surface area to hold a fax machine and printer.

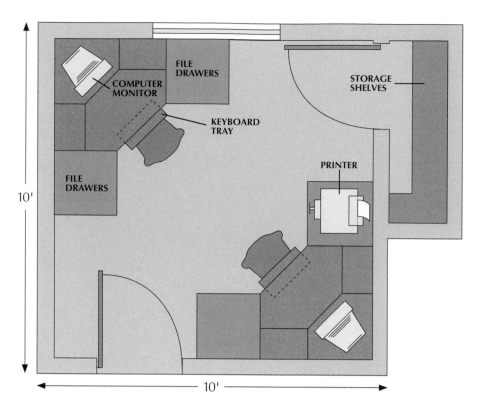

Two-person office.

With this layout two people can work comfortably in even a relatively small office. In opposite corners of the room stand identical workstations, each with file drawers, making efficient use of the space—and placing the stations back to back gives the individuals a sense of privacy. A large closet is equipped with storage shelves.

Work area for a graphic artist.

This spacious studio accommodates both the desk and drafting table needed for a graphic-design business. The U-shaped workstation includes a circular table for meetings. A counter with a file drawer along the wall accommodates a plotter. The drafting table is placed near a window, and a large cabinet in one corner stores artwork flat in large drawers and holds supplies vertically; a small table supports a color scanner.

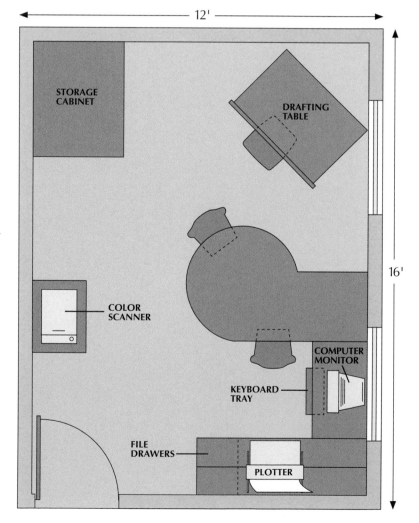

A sewing space.

This generous office houses everything needed for a sewing business. The sewing machine table sits near the window, and a small cabinet alongside accommodates supplies. A large storage unit in one corner can be used for bolts of fabric. Recessed into the wall, the ironing board can be folded down when needed, and the large cutting table on wheels can be pulled out from the wall to allow access on all sides. A small desk tucked into a corner holds a computer used for accounting purposes, and a bookcase for reference material fits behind the door.

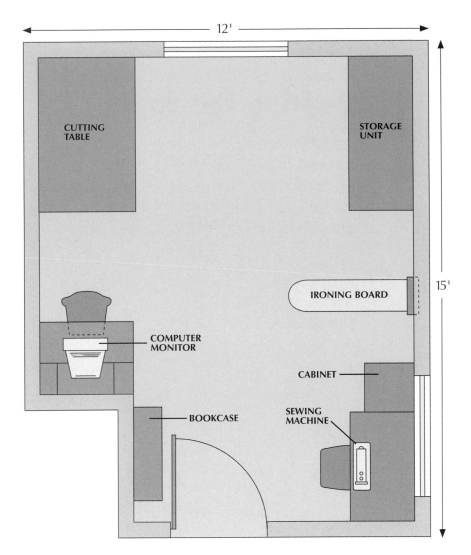

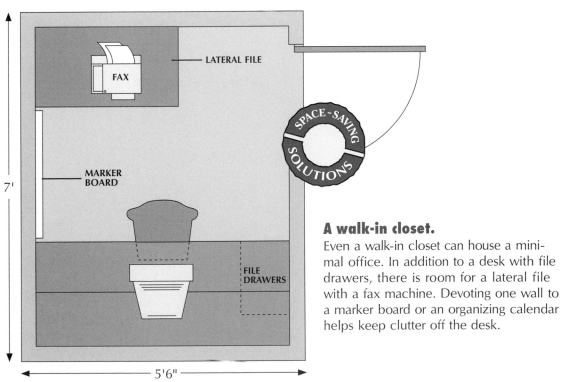

A walk-in closet.

Even a walk-in closet can house a minimal office. In addition to a desk with file drawers, there is room for a lateral file with a fax machine. Devoting one wall to a marker board or an organizing calendar helps keep clutter off the desk.

2 Adapting the Space

In a perfect world, your home would already contain a spare room just waiting for you to call it an office and set to work. Realistically, however, you may have to make do with a situation that at first seems less than ideal. You may be able to divide a large room with a new wall or partition, or open up a small room by removing a wall. Once these renovations are complete, you'll be ready to finish your new walls or ceilings.

Dividing the Space

Dividing an existing room may be the only option you have to create space for a home office. Or, if you will be setting up a large office, you may want to partition the space further, creating separate working and conference areas, for example.

New Walls: A floor-to-ceiling partition, with or without a door, is the most permanent divider *(opposite)*, one that gives you the opportunity to build in soundproofing *(page 24)*.

Another option is a half-height wall *(page 25, top)* that allows air and light to pass through. If space permits, consider adding a built-in closet for storage *(page 25, bottom)*.

New partition walls can run parallel to or perpendicular to the ceiling joists; however, if the wall will run parallel to the ceiling framing, build it directly under a joist.

Screens and Dividers: Less permanent than a partition wall, a screen can effectively fence off your office. Choose from among a variety of commercial screens or dividers, or create your own by building a frame to hold a panel of thin plywood, opaque plastic, or latticework *(pages 26-27)*.

Providing for Power: If you plan to install electrical outlets or switches in a new wall, run the wire through the studs and install the electrical boxes *(pages 63-64)* before covering the studs with wallboard.

 TOOLS

Circular saw
Combination square
Plumb bob
Hammer
Electronic stud finder

Pry bar
Utility knife
Handsaw
Staple gun
Corner clamps
Miter box
  and backsaw

 MATERIALS

1 x 3s, 2 x 4s, 2 x 6s
Common nails ($2\frac{1}{2}$", $3\frac{1}{2}$")
Finishing nails (2")
Brads ($\frac{3}{4}$")
Staples ($\frac{1}{2}$")

Cedar shims
Fiberglass insulation batts
Material for screen panels
Lattice strips ($1\frac{3}{4}$")
Wood glue
Quarter-round molding ($\frac{1}{2}$")
Decorative molding

 SAFETY TIPS

Don goggles when hammering or using a circular saw. Add gloves, long sleeves, and a dust mask when installing fiberglass insulation.

 CAUTION

Precautions for Lead and Asbestos

Lead and asbestos, known health hazards, pervade houses built or remodeled before 1978. Before cutting into walls or ceilings, check painted surfaces for lead with a test kit from a hardware store, or call your local health department or environmental protection office. To test joint compound, ceiling and wall materials, and insulation for asbestos, mist the material with a solution of 1 teaspoon of low-sudsing detergent per quart of water; then remove small samples for testing by a National Institute of Standards and Technology-certified lab.

Hire a professional who is licensed in hazardous-substance removal for large jobs indoors, or if you suffer from cardiac, respiratory, or heat-tolerance problems that may be triggered by protective clothing and a

respirator. To remove lead or asbestos yourself, follow these precautions:

▐ *Keep children, pregnant women, and animals out of the work area.*

▐ *Indoors, seal off the work area with 6-mil polyethylene sheeting and duct tape. Cover rugs and furniture that can't be removed with sheeting and tape. Turn off air-conditioning and forced-air heating systems.*

▐ *When you finish indoor work, mop the area twice, then run a vacuum cleaner equipped with a high efficiency particulate air (HEPA) filter.*

▐ *Outdoors, cover the ground in the area with 6-mil polyethylene sheeting. Never work in windy conditions.*

▐ *If you must use a power sander on lead paint, get a model equipped with a HEPA filter. Never sand asbestos-laden materials or cut them with power machinery. Mist them with water and detergent, and remove with a hand tool.*

▐ *Always wear protective clothing (available from a safety-equipment supply house or paint store) and a dual-cartridge respirator. Remove the clothing—including shoes—before leaving the work area. Wash the clothing separately, and shower and wash your hair immediately.*

▐ *Dispose of the materials you removed as recommended by your local health department or environmental protection office.*

BUILDING A PARTITION WALL

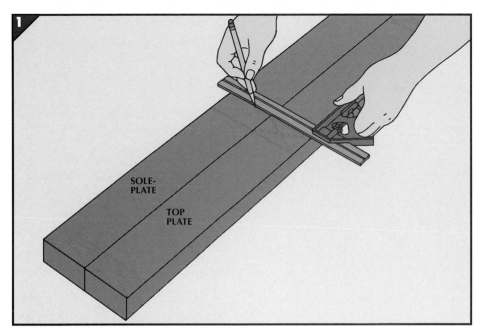

SOLE-
PLATE

TOP
PLATE

1. Marking the top and soleplates.

◆ Measure the ceiling the new wall will divide and, with a circular saw, cut two 2-by-4s to length to serve as the top and soleplates.

◆ Starting at one end of the top plate, mark stud locations $1\frac{1}{2}$ inches wide. Except at a doorway *(page 23)*, space the stud centers 16 inches apart, finishing with a stud location at the opposite end of the plate.

◆ With a combination square, transfer the markings from the top plate to the soleplate *(left)*.

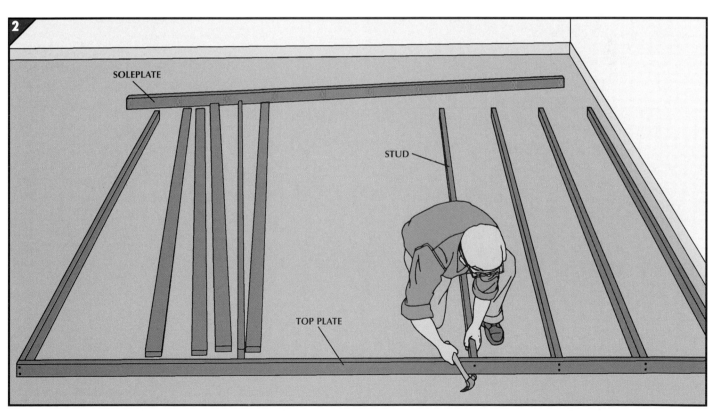

SOLEPLATE

STUD

TOP PLATE

2. Assembling the frame.

◆ To determine the stud lengths, measure along a plumb bob dropped from the ceiling to the floor at each end and in the center of the new wall.

◆ Cut 2-by-4 studs $3\frac{1}{4}$ inches shorter than the smallest of the three measurements to allow for the combined thicknesses of the top and soleplates and for ceiling clearance when raising the wall.

◆ Orient any bowed studs so they all curve in the same direction.

◆ Set the top plate on edge and fasten it to each stud with two $3\frac{1}{2}$-inch common nails driven through the plate *(above)*. A framing hammer speeds the work.

◆ Nail the soleplate to the other ends of the studs in the same way.

3. Locating the existing framing.

Use an electronic stud finder to pinpoint joists behind the ceiling where you plan to install your partition *(right)*. If the wall will cross the room perpendicular to the joists, pencil a mark at the center of each one. For a wall running directly under a joist, draw a line indicating the center of the joist.

Use the same technique to find and mark studs where the new wall will meet existing ones. If the intersection falls between studs, cut slots in the walls for nailer blocks installed about one-third and two-thirds of the way up the walls *(inset)*. Patch the slots with wallboard.

⚠️ **CAUTION** *Turn off electrical power at the service panel to all circuits in the area before cutting into the wall; check outlets on both sides of the wall to confirm that the power is off* (pages 52-53).

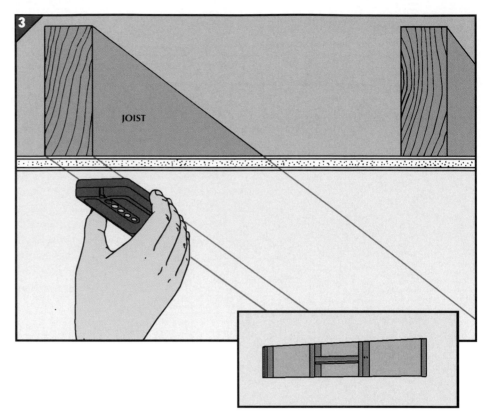

4. Removing baseboard.

For a tight fit between a new wall and an old one, remove the baseboard and shoe molding, a narrow strip often fastened at the bottom of the baseboard.

◆ Beginning at a corner or at a baseboard joint, gently loosen the baseboard and shoe molding where the new and old walls will intersect. Use a pry bar backed with a thin scrap of wood to avoid damaging the wall, and insert a wood wedge behind the baseboard to hold it away from the wall after you loosen it *(left)*.

◆ Repeat the process, inserting wedges as you go, until the strip is completely detached.

5. Securing the frame.

◆ With a helper, tilt the wall upright.

◆ While your helper holds the frame in place, push pairs of tapered cedar shims into each side of the gap between the top plate and the ceiling where you will nail the plate to joists.

◆ Drive $3\frac{1}{2}$-inch nails through the top plate and shims into the joists *(right)*; then score protruding shims with a utility knife and snap them off.

◆ Secure the soleplate to floor joists where possible; otherwise, nail it to the flooring. In either case, use $3\frac{1}{2}$-inch nails spaced 16 inches apart. For concrete floors, drive $2\frac{1}{2}$-inch cut nails.

◆ Fasten the end studs of the new wall to studs or nailer blocks in the existing ones.

FRAMING AN OPENING

A rough frame for a prehung door.

As you assemble a new partition wall *(page 21)*, frame a doorway between two king studs and adjoining jack studs, both resting on the soleplate. The jack studs support a crosspiece called a header. Short, cripple studs fit between the header and the top plate.

◆ On the soleplate mark the width of the prehung door unit, adding $\frac{1}{2}$ inch to allow for shims.

◆ Saw partway through the underside of the plate at the marks.

◆ Cut a king stud for each side of the frame and nail it to the soleplate and top plate, $1\frac{1}{2}$ inches in from the marks, with $3\frac{1}{2}$-inch common nails.

◆ For each side of the frame, cut a jack stud $1\frac{1}{4}$ inches shorter than the top of the door unit's top jamb. Nail each jack stud to the soleplate with $3\frac{1}{2}$-inch nails and to the king stud with $2\frac{1}{2}$-inch nails at 1-foot intervals.

◆ Cut a header to fit snugly between the king studs. Nail it in place with $3\frac{1}{2}$-inch nails driven through the king studs.

◆ Cut cripple studs to fit between the header and the top plate. Position these at the same intervals as the wall studs and secure them with $3\frac{1}{2}$-inch nails driven through the top plate and the header.

◆ Raise the wall into position, and complete the kerfs cut in the soleplate to remove the unwanted section.

◆ Install the door *(pages 41-43)*.

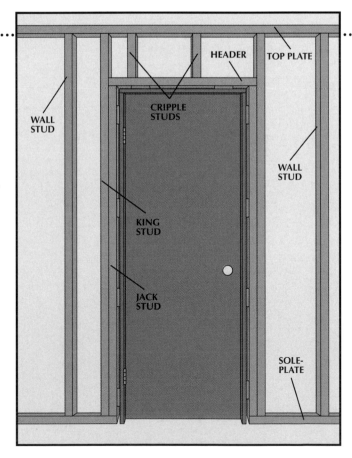

TWO WAYS TO SOUNDPROOF

Staggering the studs.
◆ Locate and mark the ceiling joists *(page 22, Step 3)*.
◆ From 2-by-6s, cut top and soleplates equal to the length of the wall.
◆ Fasten the soleplate to the floor with $3\frac{1}{2}$-inch common nails.
◆ Mark each end of the soleplate for a 2-by-6 stud, and every 12 inches in between for staggered 2-by-4 studs.
◆ With a combination square, transfer the marks to the top plate *(inset)*, then fasten the top plate to the ceiling with $3\frac{1}{2}$-inch nails.
◆ Cut studs to fit between the plates, aligning them with the marks and toenailing them in place with $3\frac{1}{2}$-inch nails.
◆ Staple batts of fiberglass insulation, $3\frac{1}{2}$ inches thick and 24 inches wide, between the wall studs *(right)*.

For additional soundproofing, install the wallboard on resilient channels *(page 40)*.

Doubling a wall.
◆ Mark the floor and ceiling for two 2-by-4 soleplates and two top plates, 1 inch apart.
◆ Cut the plates, set them side by side, and mark them for 2-by-4 studs, 16 inches on center.
◆ Fasten the top plates to the ceiling and the soleplates to the floor with $3\frac{1}{2}$-inch common nails.
◆ Toenail the studs between the plates.
◆ With $\frac{1}{2}$-inch staples, fasten 6-inch-thick batts of fiberglass insulation between the studs.

For additional soundproofing, install the wallboard on resilient channels *(page 40)*.

ERECTING A HALF WALL

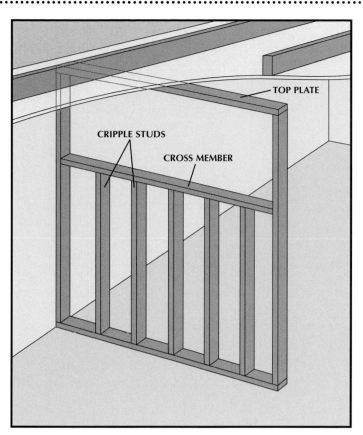

TOP PLATE

CRIPPLE STUDS

CROSS MEMBER

Constructing the new wall.

◆ Cut and assemble the top and sole-plates and the two end studs on the floor as you would for a standard partition *(page 21)*.

◆ Cut a cross member to fit between the end studs, and nail it to the studs at the desired height with $3\frac{1}{2}$-inch nails.

◆ Cut cripple studs to fit between the cross member and the soleplate, spaced 16 inches apart, and nail them in place.

◆ Raise the wall into position *(left)* and fasten it to the floor, ceiling, and existing wall as described for a standard partition wall *(page 23, Step 5)*.

ADDING A CLOSET

Framing a closet.

◆ Build and install the closet's front wall and door opening in the same way as for a partition wall *(pages 21-23)*. For easy access to the closet, you may want to frame a large opening for bifold doors *(pages 43-45)* or a set of double doors.

◆ Cut two 3-inch-long nailer blocks from 1-by-3 lumber and, with $3\frac{1}{2}$-inch common nails, fasten them to the last stud at the end of the wall that will adjoin the shorter wall.

◆ Cut a reinforcing stud and nail it to the nailer blocks. Then toenail it to the top plate and soleplate.

◆ Construct a narrow wall to fit between the new wall and the existing wall in the room.

◆ Fasten this wall in place, nailing the end stud to the nailing blocks and to the end stud of the reinforced corner.

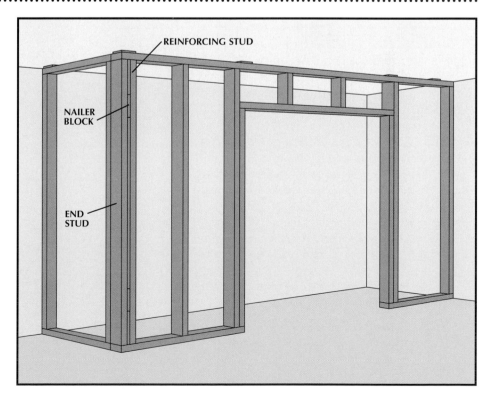

REINFORCING STUD

NAILER BLOCK

END STUD

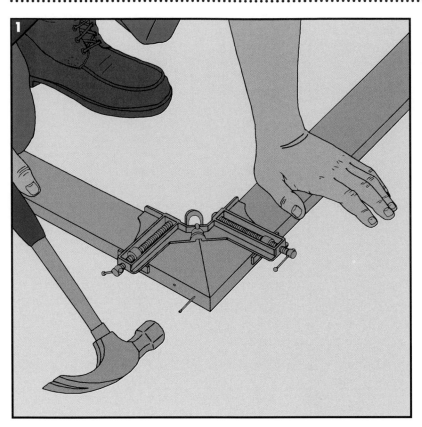

1. Constructing the frame.

To frame the screen, build a rectangle $\frac{1}{4}$ inch shorter than the height of the room so the top edge of the screen won't catch against the ceiling when you raise the divider into place. For lightweight panel materials such as plastic, use 1-by-3 lumber for the frame; for heavier materials, use 2-by-3s or 2-by-4s.

◆ Miter four lengths of lumber for the frame so the inner edges are $\frac{1}{8}$ inch longer than the dimensions of the panel.

◆ Working from corner to corner, apply wood glue to the mitered ends, then secure the frame pieces in a corner clamp.

◆ Drive 2-inch finishing nails into the joints from each direction *(left)*.

2. Tacking lattice to the frame.

If the difference between frame and panel material thicknesses is 1 inch or more, secure the panel on both sides with quarter-round molding as described in Step 3. Otherwise, proceed as follows:

◆ Scribe a guideline around the back of the frame, $\frac{7}{8}$ inch from the inner edge.

◆ Miter four $1\frac{3}{4}$-inch lattice strips so their outer edges are the same length as the scribed lines.

◆ Apply wood glue to the back of the frame between the inner edge and the scribed line.

◆ Lay the lattice strips along the line and fasten them to the frame with $\frac{3}{4}$-inch brads driven at 6-inch intervals *(right)*.

◆ Turn the frame over and insert the panel, resting it on the lattice strips.

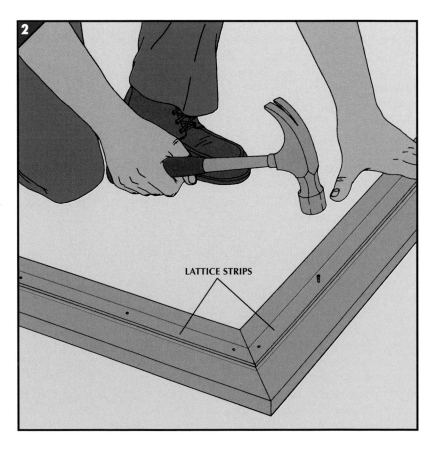

LATTICE STRIPS

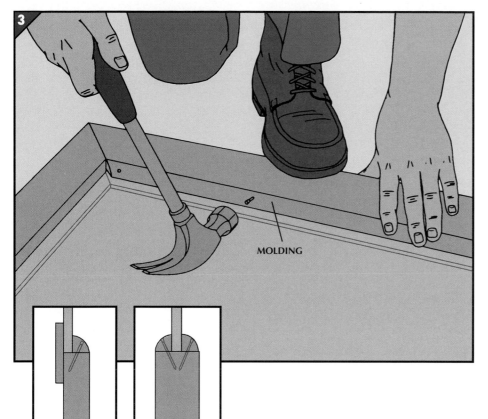

MOLDING

3. Securing the panel.

◆ Miter four lengths of $\frac{1}{2}$-inch trim such as quarter-round molding to fit the inside edges of the frame.

◆ To secure the panel, fasten the trim to the frame with glue and brads driven at an angle *(left and left inset)*.

For panels thicker than $\frac{1}{4}$ inch, secure the panel with quarter-round molding nailed to the frame on both sides *(right inset)*.

4. Securing a rectangular divider.

A three-sided, mitered channel anchors the divider to the ceiling and can also be used at the floor. To fit the divider snugly against the wall, notch either the baseboard and its shoe molding or a corner of the divider frame.

◆ For the ceiling, cut two pieces of molding that are equal in length to the width of the divider plus the thickness of its frame. With the molding in a miter box upside down, miter one end of each piece. Miter a third piece on both ends so the inside edge equals the thickness of the divider frame.

◆ Glue and nail one of the long pieces of molding to the ceiling at the panel location.

◆ Raise the divider against the molding *(right)* and nail through the molding into the divider frame.

◆ Place the second long piece of molding against the other side of the divider and then fasten it to the ceiling.

◆ Fit the short piece of molding between the ends of the longer ones *(inset)*.

At the floor, adapt the foregoing procedure or anchor the frame with nails or screws driven at an angle into the floor.

Removing Old Walls

Where you are fortunate enough to be able to devote more than one existing room to a home office, you may want to remove an intervening wall to create a sense of space.

Bearing or Nonbearing Walls: Before tearing out a wall, you must determine whether the wall bears weight from above, thus serving as a vital structural element of the house *(below)*. It is relatively easy to remove a nonbearing wall *(opposite)*—or part of one *(page 30)*. Removing a bearing wall is a project best left to professionals.

Dealing with Utilities: In making the decision to remove a wall, keep in mind that any plumbing, wiring, or ductwork will have to be rerouted. The number of receptacles and switches suggests how much wiring a wall contains. A bathroom above may be hooked to plumbing that descends through the wall. From the basement try to detect any heating pipes or ducts rising within the wall.

Finishing the Job: After removing the wall, there will be breaks in the ceiling, walls, and floor. Wallboard on ceilings and walls can be patched, and gaps in the floor can be built up with any wood as thick as the flooring, and the whole room carpeted or tiled. However, professional help may be needed for hardwood floors that will remain exposed.

⚠ **CAUTION** *Before starting work, check for lead and asbestos in the wall (page 20).*

⚠ **CAUTION** *Turn power off at the service panel to all wiring in the wall before beginning work; then test outlets on both sides of the wall (page 52) to confirm power is off.*

TOOLS

Pry bar
Circuit tester
Circular saw
Screwdriver

Handsaw
Wood chisel
Mallet
Hammer
Wallboard tools

MATERIALS

Drop cloths
Duct tape
2 x 4s

Framing lumber
Common nails ($3\frac{1}{2}$")
Wallboard materials

SAFETY TIPS

Protect yourself from the dust, flying splinters, and other debris created by demolition by putting on goggles, a dust mask, leather work gloves, long sleeves and pants, and sturdy shoes.

Bearing and nonbearing walls.

In a typical frame house, the roof is supported by long outer walls parallel to the ridge *(right)*. The weight of the remaining structure rests on joists, which transfer the load to the side walls. These walls pass the weight to the foundation and on to the footings. (End walls usually do not carry weight.) Since a standard joist cannot span the usual distance from one side wall to another, house framers provide two joists and rest their inside ends on an interior bearing wall. The interior bearing wall carries the weight down to a solid support, either to a bearing wall that rests on its own footings or, as shown here, to a girder with ends that rest on the foundation. A bearing wall can usually be identified by joists crossing its top plate, perpendicular to it, or by a girder or another wall running under and parallel to the wall. You can detect joists by looking in the attic and basement or by cutting a small hole in the ceiling. Nonbearing walls usually run parallel to the joists and perpendicular to the long walls of the house. If there is any doubt as to whether a wall bears weight, contact a qualified contractor or home inspector, or a structural engineer.

RIDGE

BEARING WALL

JOISTS

GIRDER

NONBEARING WALL

FOOTING

GETTING RID OF A NONBEARING WALL

1. Stripping the wall.
◆ Turn off the power to the circuits in the area.
◆ Tear off the wall trim *(page 22)*.
◆ Tape down drop cloths in each room, close any interior doors, and open the windows.
◆ Cut strips of wall from between the studs with a circular saw set to the thickness of the wall surface; use a metal-cutting blade if the wall is made of plaster on metal lath. Alternatively, you can break a hole in the wall material with a hammer and pull it away with a crowbar.
◆ Saw the studs in two near the middle, and work the halves free from their nailing *(right)*.
◆ When you reach an outlet, remove its cover plate and strip off the wall surface around it. Trace the cable to the nearest electrical box, disconnect it, and pull it out of the wall. If you cannot discover a cable's origin or if unrelated cables pass through the wall, consult a professional.
◆ Work the bottom of the end stud loose from the adjoining wall with a pry bar, using a wide wood scrap to protect the wall surface. When the stud is safely away from the wall, wrench it free.

DROP CLOTH

DROP CLOTH

2. The top plate and soleplates.
◆ The top plate is often nailed upward to blocks between adjacent joists. Pry it down, beginning at the nailhead nearest one end, using a wood scrap to protect the ceiling.
◆ Near the center of the soleplate, make two saw cuts about 2 inches apart.
◆ Chisel out the wood between the cuts down to the subfloor.
◆ Insert a crowbar and pry up one end of the plate *(left)*. With a scrap of 2-by-4 as a fulcrum, pry up the other end.

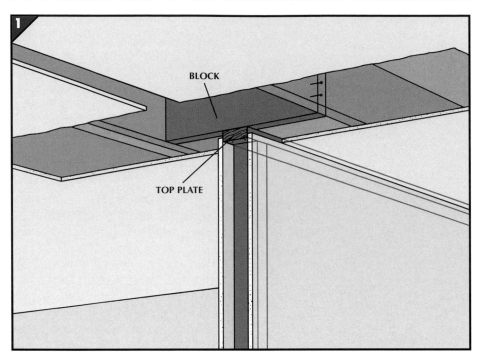

BLOCK

TOP PLATE

1. Securing the top plate.

◆ Designate a stud where you will stop demolition of the wall to preserve the remainder of it.

◆ Apply the methods on page 29 to demolish the unwanted part of the wall, but cut the wall surface and plates so they extend $1\frac{1}{2}$ inches beyond the designated stud; doing so creates a pocket for the stud to be added in Step 2.

◆ Cut a hole about 1 foot wide in the ceiling, centered on the upper end of the stud and running to the second joist on either side.

◆ Nail a block of joist-size lumber between the joists on each side of the top plate, with the face of the block flush with the end of the plate.

◆ Nail through the plate into the edge of the block *(left)*.

2. Reinforcing the stud.

◆ Cut a reinforcing stud to fit snugly between the top plate and soleplate, and nail it to the end stud in the section of the partition that you have left standing *(right)*.

◆ Surface the outer face of the reinforcing stud with wallboard and finish with corner bead *(pages 31-32 and 34)*.

The simplest way to sheath the walls of your new office is to hang sheets of wallboard—also called drywall. It consists of a gypsum core sandwiched between layers of heavy paper; a standard sheet is 4 feet wide, 8 feet long, and $\frac{1}{2}$ inch thick. Wallboard with the long edges tapered makes finishing the joints much easier.

Preparation: To calculate the number of sheets you need, determine the square footage of each wall, ignoring all openings except the largest, such as picture windows. Convert this figure into sheets by dividing it by 32, the square footage of a panel. Complete any wiring before installing the wallboard *(Chapter 3).*

Installation: Vertical seams between wallboard sheets must align with the centers of wall studs. In most cases, this is easier to accomplish when the wallboard is laid horizontally *(page 32)*; however, for a narrow wall, you can avoid creating a seam if you lay the sheet vertically. Wallboard sheets can be installed with ring-shank wallboard nails or special wallboard screws driven slightly below the surface of the panels. To create a soundproof wall, install the wallboard on resilient channels *(pages 38-40).*

Finishing the Job: Fill the holes in the wallboard left by the nail or screw heads with joint compound. Cover seams between sheets with fiberglass joint tape before applying the compound *(page 33).* Strengthen outside corners with angled metal strips called corner bead *(page 34).* Finally, paint the walls.

TOOLS

Tape measure	Caulking gun
Carpenter's square	Wallboard hammer
Utility knife	Chalk line
Hammer	Taping knives
	(6", 10")
	Wallboard sponge

MATERIALS

Wallboard	Ring-shank wallboard
Scrap 2 x 4s	nails ($1\frac{1}{2}$")
Common nails	Joint tape
($2\frac{1}{2}$")	(fiberglass and
Wallboard adhesive	precreased paper)
	Joint compound
	Metal corner bead

SAFETY TIPS

Goggles protect your eyes when you are nailing or working above eye level.

CUTTING THE SHEETS

1. Scoring wallboard.
◆ Mark a sheet of wallboard for cutting.
◆ Position a carpenter's square at the mark at one edge of the sheet and draw a line. Then move the square to the opposite edge and complete the line. (A wallboard T-square allows you to draw this line in a single stroke.)
◆ Place a square along the line and score the surface of the wallboard with a utility knife *(above).*

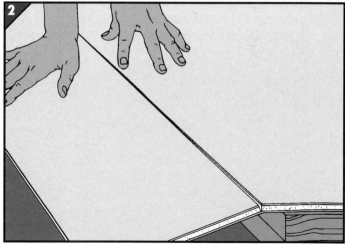

2. Snapping the core.
◆ Stack two 2-by-4 scraps under the wallboard just behind the scored line.
◆ With the palm of your hand, hit the short end of the sheet, snapping the core.
◆ Finish by slicing through the backing with a utility knife, then trim any ragged paper from the cut edge.

Putting up the panels.

◆ Mark the stud positions on the ceiling and floor.

◆ Drive $2\frac{1}{2}$-inch common nails partway into the wall studs 4 feet below the ceiling.

◆ With a caulking gun, apply a $\frac{3}{8}$-inch-thick zigzag bead of wallboard adhesive to each stud behind the sheet, starting and stopping 6 inches from the edges of the sheet.

◆ With a helper, lift the wallboard, and rest it on the nails. Align the end with the center of a stud.

◆ Nail or screw the panel to each stud about 1 foot from the ceiling. Drive the fasteners straight and flush with the surface. Then drive them slightly below the surface without breaking the paper: A wallboard hammer works well for nails; for screws, use a screw gun designed for wallboard, or a variable speed electric drill with a dimpler attachment.

◆ Add fasteners every 2 feet on each stud, ending 1 inch from the top and bottom. Double the fasteners where the centerline of the sheet crosses each stud.

◆ Because ceilings and floors are rarely parallel, measure from the bottom of the sheet to the floor in at least four places, subtract $\frac{1}{2}$ inch and mark these distances on the second sheet. If the

distances are fairly uniform, snap a chalk line between the marks, then score and break the sheet at the line *(page 31)*. If not, connect marks with separate lines and cut the sheet with a wallboard saw.

◆ Trim the second sheet to a length one stud shorter than the sheet above to create staggered joints.

◆ With a helper, raise the sheet with scrap-wood foot levers *(inset)*.

TRICKS OF THE TRADE

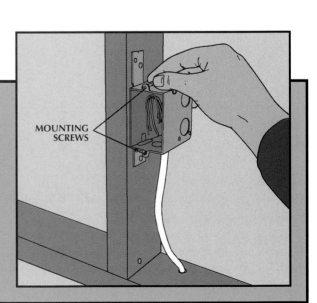

Marking for Outlet Boxes

Fold the wires into the outlet box. Remove the mounting screws and insert them from back to front through their holes so that they protrude about $\frac{1}{2}$ inch *(right)*. Place the wallboard sheet in position on the studs and press it against the screw tips. Remove the sheet and place a spare outlet box on the wallboard, aligning the mounting holes with the marks made by the screws, then trace around the box. Cut just outside the lines with a wallboard saw, angling the saw so the hole is slightly wider at the back of the sheet.

DOORS AND WINDOWS

Marking and cutting the opening.

For a window, measure from the ceiling to the top of the jamb at both corners. Then measure from the last installed sheet to the nearest side-jamb edge. If the sheet will surround the window, also measure to the farthest side-jamb edge. For a door, measure the distances from the ceiling to the top jamb and from the last installed sheet to the side-jamb edge or edges.

◆ Mark these distances on the face of the sheet and connect the marks.

◆ If the sheet will enclose three sides of the window or door, cut along the two parallel lines with a wallboard saw.

◆ Score the remaining line and snap the core *(page 31)*. If the sheet will surround a window, cut around all the lines with the saw.

◆ Mark and cut the lower sheet the same way *(right)*.

TAPING SEAMS

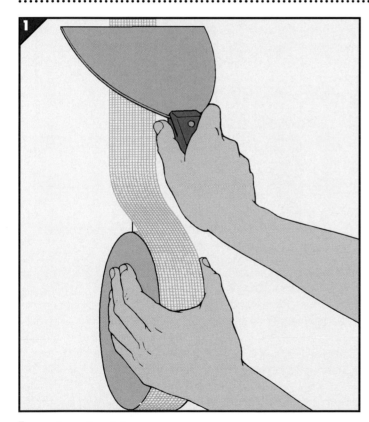

1. Taping the joint.

◆ Press the end of a roll of self-adhesive fiberglass-mesh joint tape against the top of the joint.

◆ Unwind the tape with one hand and, with a taping knife, press the tape to the joint *(above)*. Watch for wrinkles; if they appear, lift the tape, pull it tight, and press it again.

◆ Cut the tape off the roll when you reach the end of the joint.

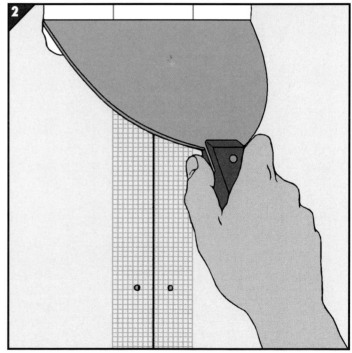

2. Applying joint compound.

◆ With the knife, spread compound over the joint tape and the adjacent wallboard in a layer approximately $\frac{1}{16}$ inch thick. On joints where nontapered ends of drywall abut, apply compound slightly thicker. While working, wipe the knife frequently against the lip of the pan so that the compound doesn't harden on the knife and score grooves in the wet compound.

◆ When the tape is covered, run the knife down the joint in one motion to smooth out the surface.

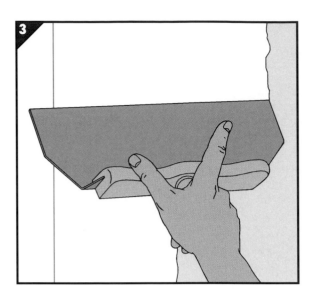

3. Feathering the joint.

◆ Run a clean 10-inch knife down each side of the joint, pressing hardest on the outer side of the knife so the mixture gradually spreads outward to a feathered edge *(left)*. Let the compound dry for a day.

◆ Hide fastener heads elsewhere by drawing joint compound across each one with a 6-inch knife held nearly parallel to the wallboard. Raise the knife blade and scrape off excess compound with a stroke at right angles to the first.

◆ Apply a second coat of compound thinned with 1 pint of water per 5 gallons. With a 10-inch knife, feather the compound to about 10 inches on either side of the joint. For nontapered ends, apply more compound, feathering it to 20 inches on each side.

◆ When the last coat of joint compound is completely dry, rub it gently with a damp wallboard sponge. Do not wet the wallboard paper enough to tear, and rinse the sponge frequently. Repeat the procedure on the compound you applied to fastener heads.

DEALING WITH CORNERS

Taping inside corners.

◆ With a 6-inch taping knife, slather joint compound crosswise into the crack at an inside corner between two walls or a wall and the ceiling.

◆ After applying the compound, run the knife along each side of the joint to smooth the surface.

◆ Bend a length of paper tape in half down its crease line, and press the fold lightly into the corner joint with your fingers *(right)*.

◆ Draw the knife along each side of the corner, simultaneously embedding the tape and coating it lightly with compound.

◆ When applying the second and third coats use thinned compound *(Step 3, above)*. Do one side of the corner, allow the compound to dry one day, then do the other side.

◆ Smooth the compound with a wallboard sponge after it has dried *(Step 3, above)*.

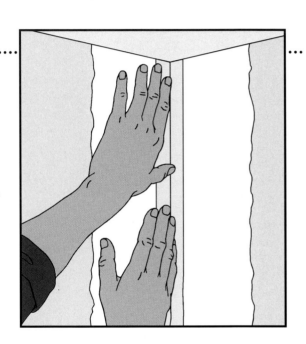

Strengthening outside corners.

◆ Nail a strip of metal corner bead so it fits flat on both sides of the corner *(left)*.

◆ Load the left two-thirds of a 6-inch taping knife with joint compound.

◆ With the right half of the blade overhanging the corner, run the knife from ceiling to floor down the left side of the bead, smoothing the compound over the perforations.

◆ Cover the right side of the bead in the same way.

◆ Clean the blade, then smooth and feather the joint by running the knife down each side of the bead.

◆ Let the compound dry for 1 day, then apply a second coat of thinned compound *(Step 3, above)*, feathering the edge about $1\frac{1}{2}$ inches beyond the dry compound.

◆ Wait 1 day, then apply a third coat using a 10-inch knife to feather the compound 2 inches farther on each side.

◆ Smooth the compound after it has dried *(Step 3, above)*. If the rounded tip of the metal bead still shows, it can be painted later with the rest of the wall.

Wallboard ceilings can be tricky to install, but they are the least expensive option, and the one most adaptable to different decorative treatments.

Planning: Sketch the layout of the sheets of wallboard carefully before the work begins *(below)*. Since electrical connections must remain accessible when the ceiling is in place, relocate existing junction boxes that would be covered by the ceiling. In addition, complete any new wiring before installing the wallboard *(Chapter 3)*.

Installation: Wallboard sheets for a ceiling are fastened the same way as those on walls—with adhesive and nails or screws *(pages 31-32)*. Cut the sheets by scoring them with a utility knife *(page 31)*; make openings with a wallboard saw.

Other Ceiling Options: Acoustic tiles and panels are more expensive than wallboard, but are easier to install *(page 37)*. Suspended panels leave wiring accessible and can be used to conceal ducts and pipes; however, they lower the height of the finished ceiling.

TOOLS

Tape measure
Circular saw
Hammer

Caulking gun
Wallboard hammer
Taping knives
  (6" and 10")
Wallboard sponge

MATERIALS

2 x 4s
Common nails (3")
Wallboard
Wallboard adhesive

Ring-shank wallboard
  nails ($1\frac{1}{2}$")
Joint tape (fiberglass and
  precreased paper)
Joint compound
Metal corner bead

SAFETY TIPS

When working overhead or when nailing, protect your eyes with goggles.

MOUNTING WALLBOARD OVERHEAD

1. Planning a wallboard ceiling.

Measure the ceiling dimensions at the top plates of the walls, and plan to install sheets perpendicular to the joists. When you diagram the ceiling, keep in mind several principles: The ends of the wallboard must be made to land at the centers of joists—by trimming the board if necessary; these joints must be staggered to prevent a continuous seam on a single joist; and any filler strips of wallboard should be installed in the center of the ceiling.

Where room dimensions create a narrow gap between the edge of a sheet and the wall, as in the L shown at right, trim back the sheet to widen the gap to at least 1 foot, and cut a piece to fill the gap. To support the edges of the wallboard if the last joist lies more than 4 inches out from the wall, install L-shaped 2-by-4 nailer blocks between the last joist and the band joist with 3-inch common nails *(inset)*. Measure and cut the sheets to fit around ceiling fixtures and other obstructions.

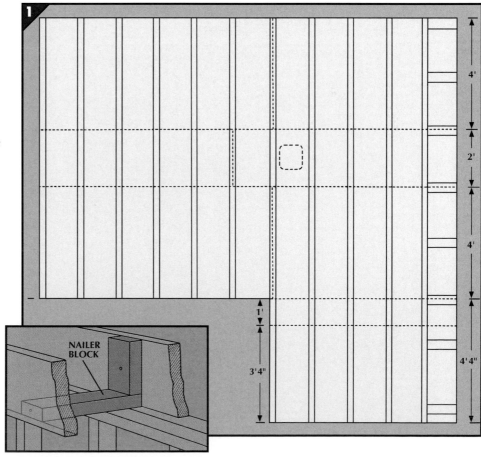

2. Marking guidelines for nails.

Make a vertical mark on the top plates below the center of each joist at both ends *(left)*, and beneath the nailer blocks if you have any. The marks will serve as guides for positioning wallboard nails after the wallboard hides the joist itself.

3. Applying adhesive.

With a caulking gun, lay $\frac{3}{8}$-inch zigzag beads of wallboard adhesive along joists that will touch wallboard *(right)*.

T-BRACE

4. Putting up the wallboard.

◆ Make a 2-by-4 T-brace the height of the ceiling and have a helper hold up the sheet while you fasten it.

◆ Place the first sheet in a corner and center its end on the joist where it will join another sheet.

◆ Secure the board with pairs of $1\frac{1}{2}$-inch ring-shank wallboard nails or screws driven into each joist at the center of the sheet *(page 32)*.

◆ Fasten the tapered sides of the panel to each joist, 1 inch from the panel edges *(left)*.

◆ Secure the panel ends with fasteners 16 inches apart and $\frac{1}{2}$ inch from the edge.

◆ Conceal the nail or screw heads with joint compound and tape the seams *(pages 33-34)*.

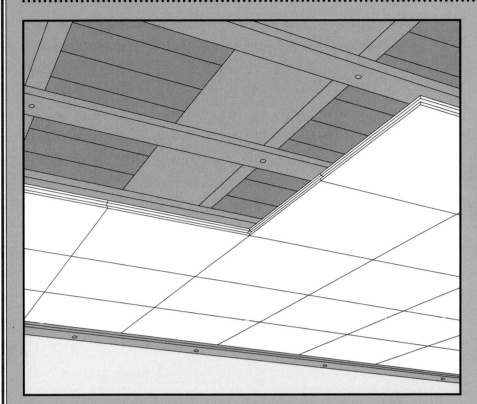

A grid of tiles.
Easy to install, acoustic tiles help absorb sound originating inside an office. They are available in kits that provide metal strips and clips for support; alternatively, tiles can be stapled to a grid of wood furring strips nailed across joists *(left)*. Tiles also can be stapled directly to an existing ceiling if it is level and free of cracks. Pipes or ducts can be hidden by building a wood frame around the obstacle, then fastening tiles to the frame.

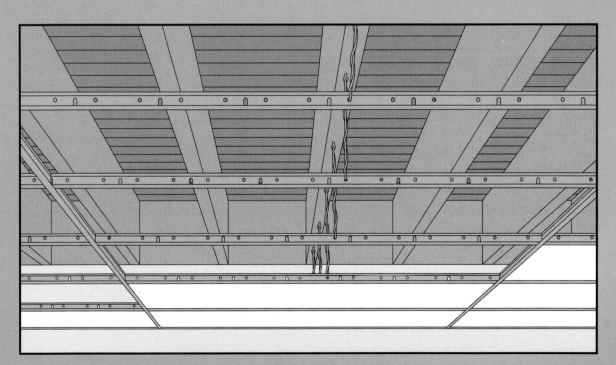

Suspended panels.
When a number of overhead pipes or ducts must be concealed—as in an unfinished basement— a ceiling made of suspended panels is the logical choice. Like acoustic tiles, panels are simple to install and serve to absorb sound in the office.

Lightweight metal runners are hung from the joists with wire; the panels are then set into the runners *(above)*. To hide ducts and pipes, runners can be hung lower to create a box around the obstruction. Fluorescent lighting panels can be substituted for regular panels.

Noise arises from two sources—sound reverberating within the room, and sound penetrating from elsewhere in the house. Sound from within can be absorbed by installing a ceiling of acoustic tiles or panels *(page 37)*, and by choosing carpet or resilient flooring as a floor covering. Exclude external noise by sealing gaps in existing walls or by soundproofing the walls themselves.

Sealing Gaps: Holes and cracks in a wall leak a surprising amount of noise: Plugging a $\frac{1}{8}$-inch-wide gap around an electrical outlet box can improve the soundproofing effectiveness of a wall by as much as 10 percent. Other ways to suppress noise include damping vibrations in heating ducts *(opposite)* and sealing gaps around doors *(below)*. Remember that forced-air heating systems often require gaps under interior doors for adequate air circulation.

Reducing Vibration: The thin, flat surface of stud-and-wallboard construction is a poor sound barrier. The flexible wallboard picks up sound vibrations and transmits them through the studs, setting in motion the wallboard on the other side. Soundproofing properties can be built into new walls by staggering the studs or by constructing two independent walls with a gap in between *(page 24)*, then filling the wall with fiberglass insulation. Two layers of wallboard can then be mounted on $\frac{1}{2}$-inch resilient metal channels, leaving a gap between the wallboard and framing; exposed ceiling joists can be treated in a similar way *(opposite and page 40)*.

The soundproofing properties of existing walls and ceilings can be improved by fastening 2-inch Z-shaped metal channels to the wall and then adding 1 inch of foam insulation and a second layer of wallboard.

Whenever walls are built out this way, electrical outlet boxes must be extended—or deeper ones installed —so that the boxes will be flush with the finished wall surface.

TOOLS

Utility knife
Hammer
Screwdriver
Staple gun

Tape measure
Chalk line
Carpenter's square
Electric drill
Caulking gun
Wallboard tools

MATERIALS

Weather stripping
Door sweep
Duct-lining kit
Fiberglass insulation
Wallboard

Cedar shims
Wallboard screws
   (1", $1\frac{1}{4}$", $1\frac{1}{2}$", $1\frac{5}{8}$")
Wallboard materials
Acoustic sealant
Resilient furring
   channels

SAFETY TIPS

Goggles protect your eyes when you are driving nails or operating power tools. Wear goggles, a dust mask, gloves, and a long-sleeved shirt to handle fiberglass insulation. Gloves are a must when working with resilient furring channels.

BLOCKING HOLES

Sealing around doors.
◆ Cut lengths of weather stripping to fit around the perimeter of the door.
◆ Hold each piece flat against the door stop so the gasket is partly compressed against the closed door. Secure the strip to the stop with the nails provided *(right)*.

To seal the gap under the door, install a sweep on the bottom of the door so the gasket is slightly compressed when the door is closed against the threshold *(inset)*. You may need to trim the door to get the right fit.

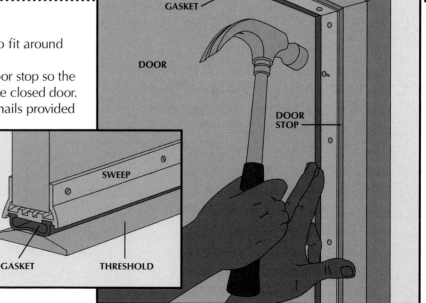

Installing duct liners.

◆ Unscrew the grille over the duct opening, then reach in and measure as far up the duct as you can.

◆ Cut acoustic duct liner to fit the measured areas and coat exposed surfaces with the adhesive sold by the liner manufacturer. Apply adhesive to the unbacked side of each piece of liner and press it into position inside the duct (*left*).

◆ Let the adhesive dry, check that the pieces are secure, then replace the grille.

SOUNDPROOFING NEW WALLS

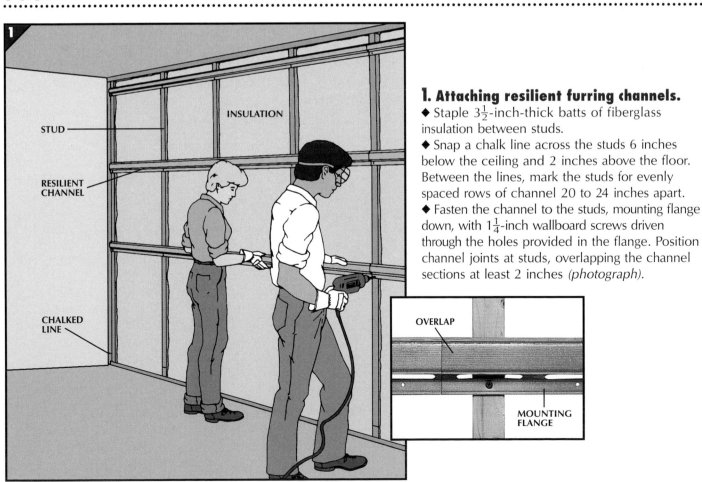

STUD

INSULATION

RESILIENT CHANNEL

CHALKED LINE

OVERLAP

MOUNTING FLANGE

1. Attaching resilient furring channels.

◆ Staple $3\frac{1}{2}$-inch-thick batts of fiberglass insulation between studs.

◆ Snap a chalk line across the studs 6 inches below the ceiling and 2 inches above the floor. Between the lines, mark the studs for evenly spaced rows of channel 20 to 24 inches apart.

◆ Fasten the channel to the studs, mounting flange down, with $1\frac{1}{4}$-inch wallboard screws driven through the holes provided in the flange. Position channel joints at studs, overlapping the channel sections at least 2 inches (*photograph*).

2. Attaching the wallboard.

Install two layers of $\frac{1}{2}$-inch wallboard panels, the first layer vertically, and the second horizontally.

◆ Trim the panels for the first layer $\frac{1}{4}$ inch shorter than the ceiling height (*page 31*).

◆ Shim the first panel to support it $\frac{1}{8}$ inch above the floor, then fasten it to the channels with 1-inch, fine-thread wallboard screws at 24-inch intervals.

◆ Remove the shims and use them to install the rest of the first layer, leaving a $\frac{1}{8}$-inch gap between panels (*right*).

◆ Caulk the gaps between panels and at the floor and ceiling with acoustic sealant (*inset*).

◆ Install the second layer of wallboard, duplicating the $\frac{1}{8}$-inch gaps of the first layer, but using $1\frac{5}{8}$-inch wallboard screws spaced 16 inches apart.

◆ Caulk the gaps with acoustic sealant.

◆ Complete the joints between panels and at the corners and ceiling with tape and joint compound (*pages 33-34*).

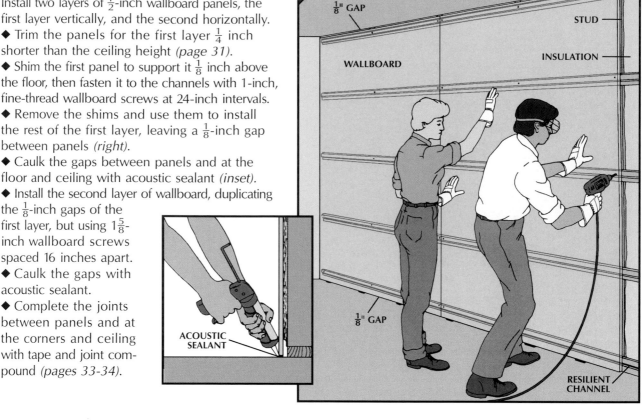

A SOUNDPROOF COVERING FOR EXPOSED JOISTS

Soundproofing a ceiling.

◆ Install 6-inch-thick batts of fiberglass insulation between the exposed joists and against the subfloor above, stapling the batts to the sides of the joists at 2- to 3-inch intervals.

◆ Fasten resilient furring channels across the exposed joists, overlapping the channels by 2 inches, and fastening them with a $1\frac{1}{2}$-inch wallboard screw at each joist (*left*).

◆ Fasten wallboard panels across the resilient channels with 1-inch wallboard screws, leaving a $\frac{1}{8}$-inch gap around the perimeter of the ceiling. Center joints between panels on channel flanges and fasten the panels to the channels with 1-inch fine-threaded wallboard screws at 24-inch intervals.

◆ Caulk all the gaps with an acoustic sealant and tape the seams (*pages 33-34*).

Hanging a Door

The traditional way to provide access to your new office is to install a prehung door. However, if your office space has a very wide entry, you'll need to consider other options such as accordion, sliding, or bifold doors. Bifold doors are an attractive solution. They open and close easily, and can be left ajar to let in light, or closed to hide the work area. They are also a good choice for a large closet converted to an office.

Prehung Doors: The simplest type to install is a split-jamb model. These units consist of two preassembled sections that are slipped between the jack studs of the rough opening *(pages 41-42)* from opposite sides to sandwich the wall. However, for a more soundproof barrier, you can install a solid-core door, available prehung but without integral casing.

When you order a door from a lumberyard, you must specify the width of the jamb (the thickness of the wall) and the width of the finished door. You must also specify whether you want the door to open clockwise in top view (a right-handed door) or counterclockwise.

Bifold Doors: Available as solid panels or with louvered ones that permit ventilation when they are closed, bifold doors consist of panels hinged together lengthwise in pairs. One or more pairs of panels can be mounted at one side of the door opening and pulled all the way across it; more commonly, however, a pair of panels is installed at each side of the opening and brought together at the middle *(pages 43-45)*.

TOOLS

Carpenter's level
Flush-cutting saw
Hammer
Utility knife
Nail set
Putty knife
Hacksaw
Electric drill
Screwdriver
Plumb bob

MATERIALS

Split-jamb door
Shims
Finishing nails
   $(1\frac{1}{2}", 2", 3\frac{1}{2}")$
Wood putty
   or spackling
   compound
Bifold door and
   hardware kit

SAFETY TIPS

Always wear goggles to protect your eyes when hammering.

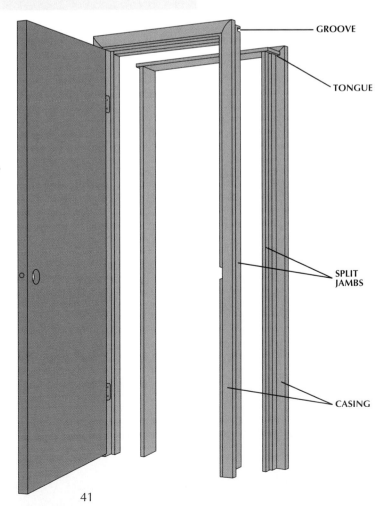

An interior split-jamb door.
This door unit has two jamb sections that fit together with a tongue-and-groove joint *(right)*. The casing, or visible trim, on both sections is factory-installed.

GROOVE

TONGUE

SPLIT
JAMBS

CASING

INSTALLING A SPLIT-JAMB DOOR

1. Installing the door.
◆ Slide the jamb section containing the door into the rough opening, resting the door on two pairs of shims. Insert pairs of shims behind the side jambs at the heights of the hinges.

◆ Adjust the shims behind the hinge-side jamb until the jamb is plumb *(right)*.

◆ If the gap between the lock-side corner of the head jamb and the door is more than $\frac{1}{8}$ inch, trim the bottom of the lock-side jamb by about $\frac{1}{16}$ inch; leave the door in place and use a flush-cutting saw *(photograph)*.

◆ Nail the hinge-side casing to the wall with $1\frac{1}{2}$-inch finishing nails into the jamb and 2-inch nails into the framing.

2. Adjusting the casing.
◆ With a $\frac{1}{8}$-inch gauge such as a piece of corrugated cardboard, adjust the top casing until there is a $\frac{1}{8}$-inch gap between the head jamb and the door, then nail the casing to the header with 2-inch finishing nails *(left)*.

◆ Adjust the gap between the door and the lock-side jamb in the same way, and nail the lock-side casing.

◆ From the other side of the door, insert pairs of shims above the head jamb, behind the middle of the hinge-side jamb, and behind the lock-side jamb.

◆ Drive two $3\frac{1}{2}$-inch finishing nails through each pair.

◆ Score the shims with a utility knife, then break them off flush with the edge of the jambs.

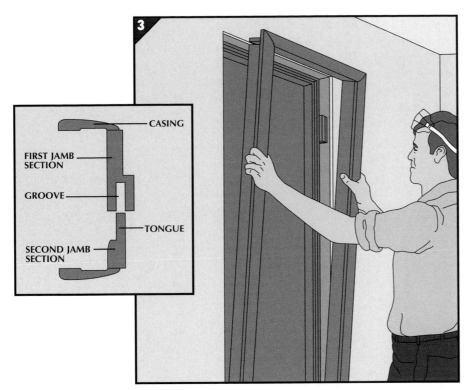

FIRST JAMB SECTION

CASING

GROOVE

TONGUE

SECOND JAMB SECTION

3. Finishing the jamb installation.

◆ Fit the tongue of the second jamb section into the groove of the first one *(inset)*, then push the second section inward until the attached casing rests against the wallboard *(left)*.
◆ Fasten the casing as in Step 1 *(opposite)*.
◆ Drive $3\frac{1}{2}$-inch finishing nails through the second jamb section and the shims into the rough framing.
◆ Set all the nails and, with a putty knife, fill the holes with wood putty—if you intend to stain the casing—or spackling compound.

PUTTING IN BIFOLD DOORS

TRACK

1. Mounting the track.

◆ Measure the width of the top of the opening and the length of the track, which should be $\frac{1}{8}$ inch shorter. If necessary, cut the track to size with a hacksaw.
◆ Center the track at the top of the opening and mark the screw holes; set the track aside.
◆ Drill pilot holes to match the screws provided with the kit.
◆ Attach the track *(right)*.

2. Installing the bottom bracket.

◆ From the center of the top pivot bracket (which comes attached to the track), drop a plumb line to the floor *(left)* and lightly mark the floor at the indicated point.

◆ Set the bottom pivot bracket *(photograph)* in place against the side wall of the opening, with the floor mark centered between the sides of the notched slot.

◆ Drill pilot holes for the screws provided; screw the bottom bracket to the wall and the floor.

For a two-door set, follow the same procedure on the opposite side of the opening.

3. Preparing the door.

◆ With a hammer, gently seat the bottom pivot in the hole at the bottom of the door panel nearest the wall.

◆ Follow the same procedure to insert the top pivot into the hole at the top of that door panel, and the roller guide into the hole at the top of the other panel. Both the top pivot and the roller guide are spring-loaded to simplify installation.

◆ Fold the door and slip the top pivot into the top pivot bracket *(right and top inset)*. Push the door upward to compress the top pivot and insert the bottom pivot into its bracket *(bottom inset)*.

◆ Unfold the door, hold down the spring-mounted roller guide, and slip it into the track.

For a two-door set, install the other door in the same way.

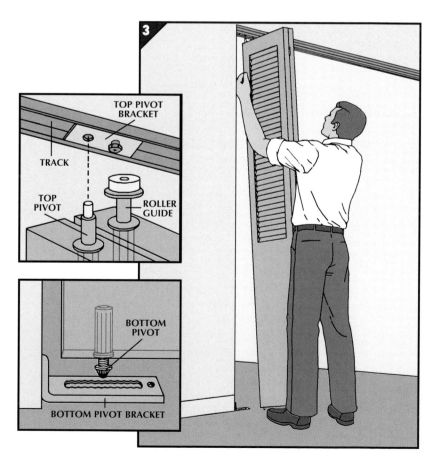

4. Securing the snugger.

Insert the snugger into the track *(left)*. For a single door, place the snugger between the roller guide and the top pivot; in the case of a two-door set, put the snugger between the doors.

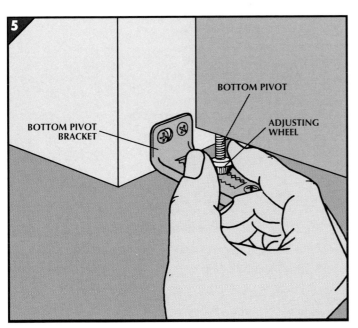

5. Adjusting the doors.

To raise or lower a door slightly, note which notch the bottom pivot occupies in its bracket. Then lift out the pivot and turn the adjusting wheel—counterclockwise to lower the door, clockwise to elevate it *(left)*. Reseat the pivot in the correct notch.

You can move the bottom of a door sideways by lifting the bottom pivot and moving it to another notch.

To shift the top of a door, remove the door, loosen the screw holding the top pivot bracket, and move the bracket. Retighten the screw and replace the door.

After positioning the doors so that they align well, attach the handles.

6. Mounting the aligners.

Bifold doors mounted on each side of an opening and meeting in the middle when closed are usually held flush and in line with metal aligners. To install the aligners, mount one on the back of each closed door *(right)*. You can fine-tune the position of each aligner by loosening the screws and sliding the aligner along the adjustment slots.

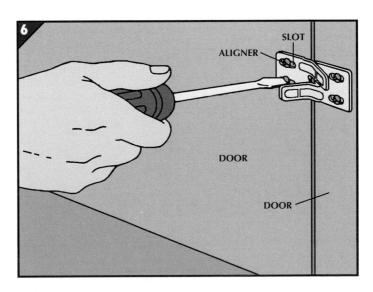

Wiring for the Home Office

When your house was built, no one could have anticipated the electrical requirements of a home office. Your chosen space will require outlets for plugging in computers and printers, fax machines and photocopiers—you may even need to add new circuits. You'll also be needing more extensive and more versatile lighting, and you may need to modify or upgrade your present telephone system.

Clamping cable to an electrical box →

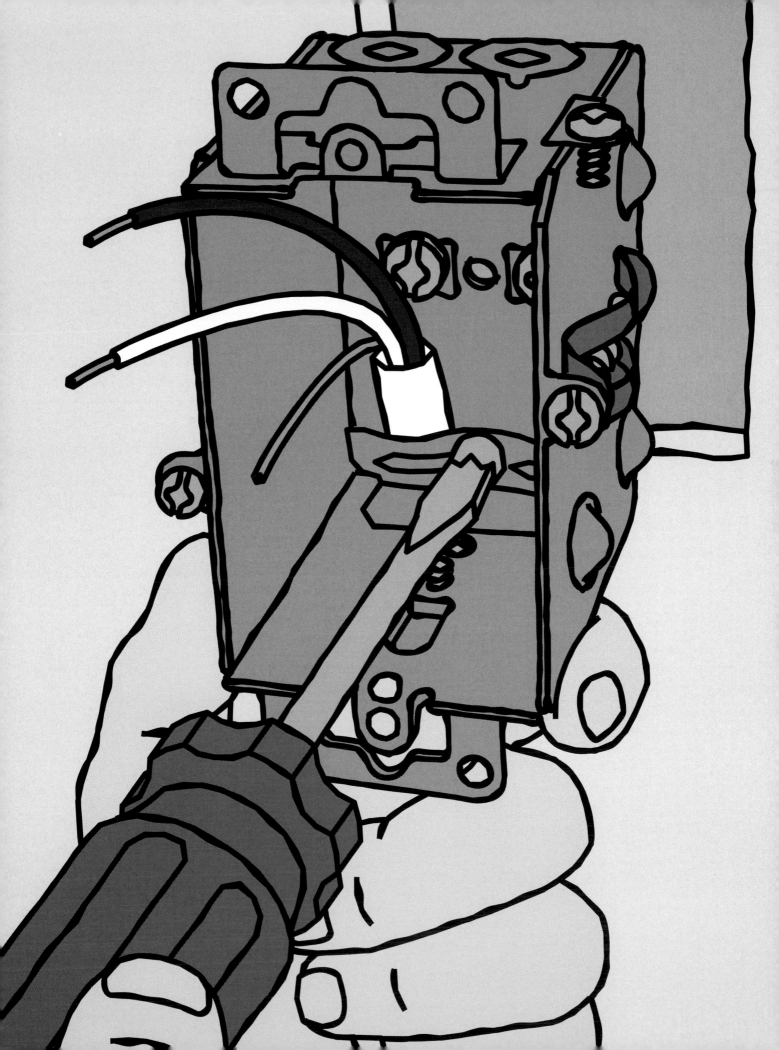

Wiring Needs

Today's fully equipped office, with its wide array of electronic equipment, and lighting, heating, and ventilation needs, can place heavy demands on a home's electrical system. Adding new outlet boxes to your office may be adequate to serve your needs *(pages 61-66)*; however, you may need to install new circuits to avoid overloading the existing ones *(pages 54-60)*. The amount of current each piece of equipment draws is generally indicated in amps on the device—if indicated in watts, divide the watts by the circuit's voltage to obtain the amperage. Consult the chart *(right)* for typical ratings so you can anticipate the electrical needs of new equipment.

Electronic Safeguards: Protect any sensitive electronic apparatus from power fluctuations by plugging it into a circuit that serves no equipment with a motor that cycles on and off, such as refrigerators. To avoid voltage surges, keep microwave ovens and coffeemakers on a circuit separate from electronic equipment. In addition, items that need to be shielded from power spikes can be hooked up to a surge protector. (Some surge protectors also provide protection for telephone lines.) You may want to provide some equipment with an uninterruptible power supply, or UPS *(opposite, bottom)*. The chart at right suggests the type of backup device each piece requires.

Lighting: As you plan new electrical circuits for your home office, try to anticipate your lighting needs *(page 51)*. Light fixtures can generally be wired to the same circuit as computer equipment.

Other Equipment: Include any proposed heating, cooling, and ventilation apparatus in your wiring plan. Air conditioners and electric baseboard heaters that are permanently wired to the house circuitry require their own separate circuits *(page 50)*.

POWER REQUIREMENTS FOR OFFICE EQUIPMENT

Equipment	Amps	Surge Protection	UPS
Answering machine	0.1	no	no
CD-ROM drive, external	0.2	yes	yes
Computer with 300-watt supply	2.7	yes	yes
Disk drive, external	0.2	yes	yes
Disk drive, removable	0.2	yes	yes
Fax machine	1.5	yes	no
Lamp	0.5	no	no
Modem, external	0.1	yes	yes
Monitor, 14" to 15"	1.5	yes	yes
Monitor, 17"	1.9	yes	yes
Monitor, 20"	2.4	yes	yes
Photocopier, desktop	8.0	no	no
Plotter	2.0	yes	no
Printer, medium laser	7.6	no	no
Printer, personal laser	6.0	no	no
Printer, ink jet	0.4	no	no
Printer, dot matrix	1.0	no	no
Scanner	1.5	yes	no
Speakers, self-powered	0.1	yes	no

Calculating the load on a circuit.

The chart above shows the amperage drawn by typical office equipment. Add up the amps drawn by all the equipment on a circuit that might be running at the same time. To avoid overloading a 15-amp circuit, the total cannot exceed 12 amps; for a 20-amp circuit, the maximum is 16 amps. The chart also indicates whether surge protection or an uninterruptible power supply is recommended.

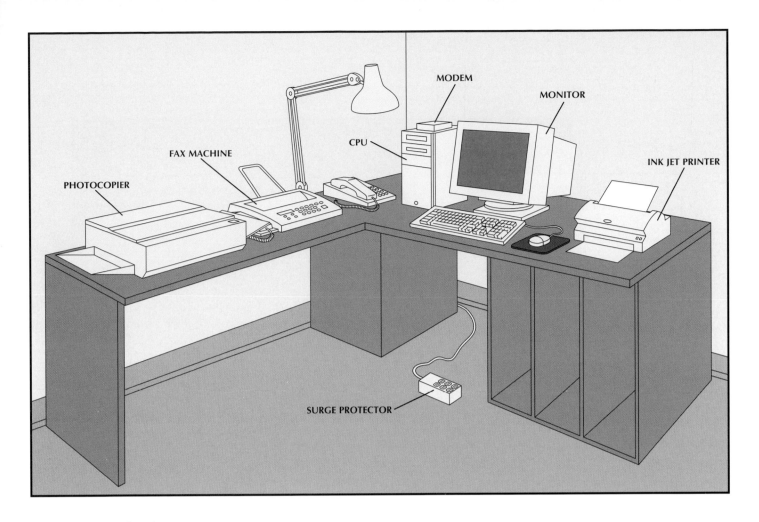

FAX MACHINE

PHOTOCOPIER

MODEM

MONITOR

CPU

INK JET PRINTER

SURGE PROTECTOR

Planning the circuits.

Except for the copier, telephone, and lamp, all the office equipment shown here requires surge protection. For convenience, it can be connected to the same circuit by way of a multireceptacle surge protector. However, laser printers, photocopiers, and other big power users require a circuit of their own.

UNINTERRUPTIBLE POWER SUPPLIES

If you live in an area subject to frequent power outages, consider plugging your computer equipment and peripherals into an uninterruptible power supply (UPS). In the event of an outage—or the power drop that is common in older buildings—the device provides power long enough for you to save your work and shut down the computer. Depending on the model, a UPS may provide backup power up to 30 minutes. To determine which equipment benefits from a UPS, consult the chart opposite.

Buy a model with a sufficient number of receptacles for your current and anticipated future needs, and check that the unit's power cord is long enough. Some UPS units offer protection for an entire computer network, but this is seldom necessary for a home office.

Most units incorporate surge protection, so you can also plug any equipment needing surge protection into a UPS.

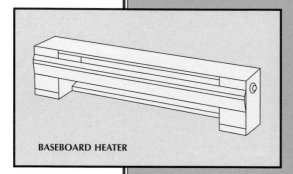

BASEBOARD HEATER

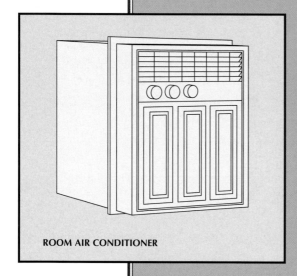

ROOM AIR CONDITIONER

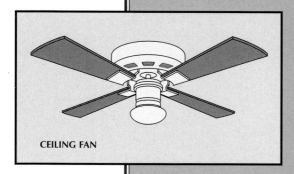

CEILING FAN

If your office is in a room of your home, its temperature will likely be comfortable. For a newly finished room in a basement or attic, you may be able to tap into the existing heating and cooling system. When this is not possible, you will need to provide independent heat and air-conditioning, which must be taken into account in your wiring plan.

A simple heat source to install is a baseboard heater. Some small units can be plugged into a wall receptacle, provided the receptacle is on an independent circuit. To obtain more heating capacity, buy a direct-wired model; 120-volt heaters are available, but 240-volt units are more common. To install the unit on a wall, remove the baseboard and fasten the heater to the wall. You'll need to run cable for a circuit to the wall and connect the cable to the heater's wires. If you don't feel comfortable doing this work yourself, consult an electrician; and always have an electrician hook up the cable to the service panel.

To cool an office, a room air conditioner is a good choice. Check the power requirement for your model and run a dedicated circuit for the air conditioner; depending on the model, a 240-volt circuit may be required. Also check the type of receptacle required— some air conditioners require a special one—and locate the outlet box as close as possible to the window. In some areas, you may be permitted to wire an air conditioner and a heater to the same circuit—check your local codes.

A ceiling fan will help keep the air moving in a room. Frugal in its electrical needs—a unit can be on the same circuit as the lighting fixtures in a room—and will increase the efficiency of your heating and cooling system. Some models also incorporate a light fixture. A fan can be hooked up to an existing ceiling outlet box, or you may want to choose a new location. Fans are heavy, so use a metal box approved for this use and attach it securely to the ceiling joists.

Lighting Requirements

Working without adequate light or with the wrong kind of light can cause eyestrain, headaches, and drowsiness. Your lighting plan should provide for two types of light—ambient and task. When buying light fixtures, also consider the type of bulb they take.

Ambient Lighting: An office requires a certain level of gentle, diffuse light. Light from a window, skylight, or glass door gives the most comfortable light to work by. Ambient light can also be provided by suspended or recessed lights *(pages 68-72)*. Wall or ceiling fixtures that point up to bounce light off the ceiling provide indirect lighting with little shadow. Track lights do not generally diffuse light evenly enough for working environments.

Task Lighting: Light that is directed to the working area can be provided by desktop lamps or by lamps attached to a wall or shelf above a desk and pointed downward. Small, specially designed halogen or fluorescent fixtures mounted under a shelf over a work surface also provide good task lighting. Ceiling fixtures are not a good source of task lighting because they cast shadows as you bend over your work.

Although most task lights are designed to be movable, it is best to plan their locations so you can place outlets nearby, avoiding a tangled mess of wires.

Types of Bulbs: Incandescent light bulbs are the most common type of lamp. They have a shorter life expectancy and are less energy efficient than other types of bulbs; however, long-life and reduced wattage bulbs are available.

Halogen bulbs, a type of incandescent lamp, produce a brighter, whiter light than regular incandescents, and are also somewhat more energy-efficient. Halogen bulbs require a special type of fixture that includes a transformer.

Fluorescents are the longest-lasting as well as the most energy-efficient bulb. While they often produce a cold bluish light, there are types that produce a warmer light. Regular fluorescent tubes require a special fixture that includes a ballast, but some compact fluorescents can be used in an incandescent fixture.

A well-lit office.
In this office, a large window admits ample natural light; the computer's screen is placed at a right angle to the window to reduce glare. Depending on the direction the window faces, blinds may be required. A wall fixture pointed at the ceiling supplements the natural light from the window, and task lights direct light onto the drafting table and desk.

Wiring Essentials

Working with wiring is not dangerous, provided that you follow all the safety rules and take the time to do the job correctly. Before beginning any wiring job, make sure you are well versed with the basics of how a home electrical system works, as well as familiar with all the safety tips given below. If you are at all uncertain of the techniques, hire a professional.

Working to Code: Local electrical codes, which have the force of law, govern the type and size of all electrical equipment as well as installation methods. You must be familiar with your local code before starting any wiring job. Also ask the building authorities whether you need a permit and what kinds of inspections will be required during and after the work. Some jurisdictions allow only licensed electricians to work on home wiring.

Volts, Amps, and Watts: Voltage is the measure of the "force" in a circuit. Normally, house circuits carry 120 volts, but some large appliances may require 240 volts. Amps measure the amount of current actually flowing in a circuit. Most house circuits carry 15 or 20 amps; determine your wiring needs according to the equipment you plan to install *(page 48)*.

Grounding: A typical circuit has two conductors. Wires encased in black insulation carry current from the service panel to the outlet boxes; white wires return it to the service panel and from there to the earth, or ground. Fire or electric shock may occur if current leaks from a black (hot) wire to a metal fixture. A person touching the fixture can conduct the current to ground, with possibly fatal consequences. For this reason, electrical cable must include a third wire, usually bare copper, to provide a safe path to ground. Every receptacle, switch, light fixture, and metal outlet box in a house must be grounded by a wire connected to this copper wire. If you find an ungrounded outlet box, consult an electrician.

Choosing Cable: The three wires bundled together in standard cable vary in size according to the amount of amperage they are designed to carry—too small a wire can overheat, possibly melt its insulation and cause a fire. Select No. 12 cable for a 20-amp circuit, or No. 14 for a 15-amp circuit.

Cutting the Power: Never work on an outlet box or cut into a wall without being certain that the circuit is off. First, flip the breaker or pull the fuse for the circuit at the service panel. Insert the probes of a voltage tester into the vertical slots of a receptacle served by the circuit; if the tester glows, the power is still on. Where there is any doubt, turn off all the circuits at the service panel. Before working directly on a fixture, switch, or receptacle, check again with a voltage tester after removing the cover plate *(opposite)*.

Making Connections: All electrical connections must be made in an outlet box. First remove about 10 inches of the outer insulation from the cable with a cable ripper, being careful not to damage the insulation of the individual wires. Then remove about $\frac{1}{2}$ inch of insulation from each wire with a wire stripper. Join wires with plastic wire caps, available in a variety of sizes; ensuring that the cap completely hides the bare wire.

Checking the Work: With the job done and the power still off, check for short circuits with a continuity tester. First unscrew any light bulbs on the circuit, then touch the tester's alligator clip to the black wire in the circuit's last box. Touch the other probe to the white wire, then to the bare copper wire, and finally to the box itself. A glowing tester bulb in any of these cases indicates a short circuit: Check any new connections for damaged insulation or bare wires contacting each other and make the necessary corrections. Mount cover plates over receptacles and switches. Once you've replaced the cover plate, turn the power and check a receptacle for power with a voltage tester.

Electrical Safety Tips

✔ Never work on a live circuit. Until you have determined the circuit is off, assume it is live—work carefully to avoid touching any screw terminals or bare wire.

✔ When turning off power as described above, stand on a dry surface and use only one hand.

✔ Do not touch a sparking, blackened, or rusted service panel. Never work on the wiring inside it.

✔ Label or lock the service panel so no one will turn the power back on by mistake while you are working on the electrical system.

✔ Never work on wiring in wet conditions or with wet hands, feet, or hair.

✔ Do not touch a metal pipe or any other potential conductor when you are working on wiring.

TESTING FOR POWER

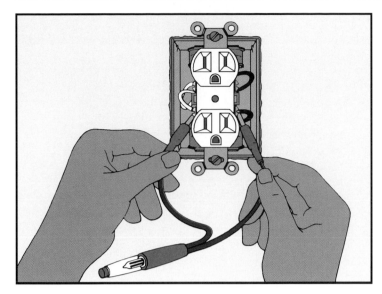

Testing a receptacle for power.

Before working, turn off power to the circuit at the service panel and make the following checks with a voltage tester. If the tester's neon bulb glows at any stage of the process, the circuit still has power; stop and try a different fuse or circuit breaker at the service panel.

◆ Before removing the cover plate, check that power is off by inserting the probes of a voltage tester into the receptacle's vertical slots.

◆ Remove the cover plate. Working carefully to keep your hands away from any bare wires or metal parts, touch the probes to the terminal screws where the black and white wires attach to the receptacle *(left)*. On a dual receptacle, test both pairs of terminals.

◆ Test from each black wire to the ground wire to check for defects or improper wiring in the neutral circuit.

Testing a switch for power.

◆ To verify that electricity to a switch has been shut off, unscrew the cover plate, then the switch. Pull the switch from the box by the mounting strap.

◆ Working carefully to keep your hands away from any bare wires or metal parts, touch one probe of a voltage tester to the outlet box if it is metal—or to the ground wire if the box is plastic—and touch the other probe to each of the brass terminals on the switch. The tester's bulb will not glow if electricity to the switch has been turned off.

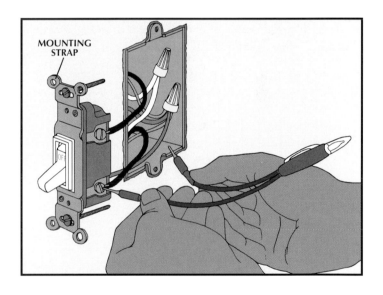

MOUNTING STRAP

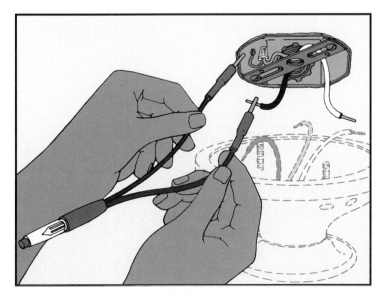

Checking a light fixture.

◆ Turn off power to the fixture at the service panel. Flip the wall switch to OFF.

◆ Unscrew the fixture and pull it away from the box to expose the wires.

◆ Hold the fixture in one hand and remove the wire caps with the other. Work carefully to avoid touching any bare wires or metal parts. Keep black and white wires away from each other and from the box if it is metal.

◆ Gently loosen each fixture wire from the corresponding house wire. Set the fixture aside.

◆ In the following checks, a voltage tester will not glow if the power is off: Touch one probe of the tester to the black wire in the box and the other to ground—the box if it is metal *(left)*, or the ground wire in a plastic box. Check also for voltage between the black wire and the white wire and between the white wire and ground.

Extending or Adding Circuits

To equip your new office with sufficient receptacles, as well as outlet boxes for light fixtures, you may be able to simply extend an existing circuit. However, if the equipment you plan to power will overload the circuit, or if you want separate circuits for computer equipment *(pages 48-49)*, you will need to add new circuits. The steps for extending or adding a circuit are essentially the same except that in one case you tap into a circuit at an existing outlet box, and in the other you run the cable directly from the service panel.

Locating the New Boxes: Turn off power to all circuits in the room. Select a location for the first new box and, if the room is already finished, make an opening for it in the wall or ceiling *(pages 56-57)*.

Routing the Cable: If you're tapping into an existing circuit, find a box as close to the new box site as possible to provide power for the extension. Only certain types of boxes can be rewired for an extension *(below)*. If your cable must be routed behind the ceiling, try to tap into a box that allows you to run the cable along, rather than across, the joists.

Draw a map of the room showing the existing box or service panel, the new box, and the positions of studs and joists. This will help you plan a route for running the new cable. You can then estimate how much cable you will need. Provide 8 extra inches of cable for each box, and add another 20 percent to allow for unexpected deviations in the cable's route.

To run the cable, cut access holes in walls and ceilings, drill a path for cable through studs or joists, and fish the cable through *(pages 58-60)*; or run it along the surface *(pages 61-62)*.

Hooking Up: With the new cable in place, clamp it to the new box and install the box *(pages 64-66*. Connect the cable to the switch or receptacle *(pages 66-67)*, or install the light fixture *(pages 68-72)*. Then, for an extension, hook up the cable to the existing box following the diagrams opposite. For new circuits, have an electrician hook up the cable to the service panel.

Wrapping Up: Once the job is done, carefully check your work *(page 52)*. Then, shut off the power again and patch the holes you made in the walls or the ceilings. Finally, turn the power back on. Your new circuit is ready for use.

HOW A BOX IS WIRED

Close inspection of an existing box will reveal whether it is a good candidate for extension. After shutting off the power at the service panel, remove the cover plate on the box and determine the type of box and the number of connections it already contains. Middle-of-the-run switch and outlet boxes—identified by the two cables, one incoming and one outgoing, clamped to them—can easily be extended. So can end-of-the-run receptacles, identified by their single incoming cable. However, end-of-the-run switches, which are also attached to only one cable, cannot serve as circuit extenders. Nor can any outlet box controlled by a wall switch, since the switch would then control the entire extension.

Most boxes are wired with 14-gauge cable. If the box contains only one or two such cables, a second or third can be added. In a kitchen area, receptacle boxes may contain thicker 12-gauge cable. In a box with only one 12-gauge cable, a second can be added. If you are unsure of the type of cable, or for a box containing more than one switch or receptacle, consult your local building department.

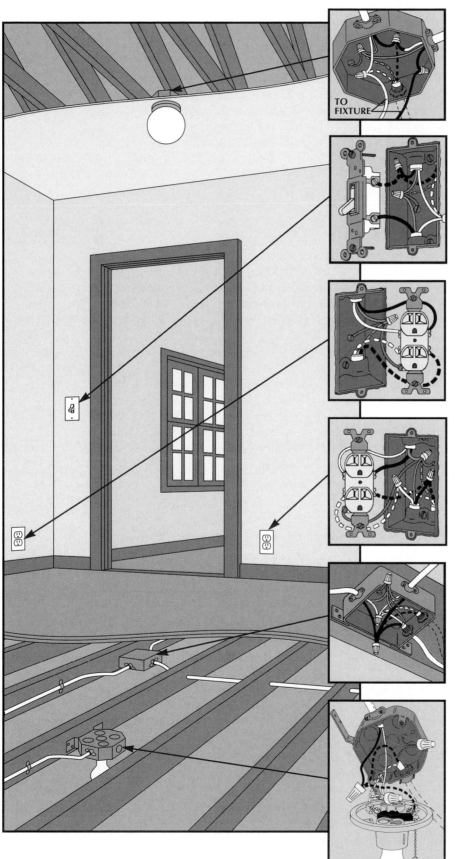

Middle-of-the-run ceiling box.

Attach the black, white, and ground wires of the new cable *(dashed lines)* to the corresponding wires in the cable bringing power from the service panel.

Middle-of-the-run switch.

Disconnect the incoming black wire from the switch terminal and join it to the black wire from the new cable and a black jumper *(dashed lines)*. Connect the jumper to the switch terminal. Attach the new white and ground wires *(dashed lines)* to the corresponding wires already in the box.

End-of-the-run receptacle.

Attach the black and white wires of the new cable *(dashed lines)* to the unused terminals on the receptacle. Connect the new ground wire *(dashed line)* to the existing ground wire and to the jumper.

Middle-of-the-run receptacle.

Remove a black wire from a receptacle terminal and join it with both the black wire of the new cable and a black jumper *(dashed lines)*. Attach the jumper to the terminal. Repeat for the white wires. Attach the new ground wire *(dashed line)* to the other ground wires and the green jumper.

Junction box.

After identifying the cable from the circuit you wish to extend, attach the black, white, and ground wires of the cable to the new cable's corresponding wires *(dashed lines)*.

End-of-the-run pull-chain fixture.

Disconnect the black and white wires. Join each to its corresponding wire in the new cable and to a jumper *(dashed lines)*. Attach the black jumper to the brass-colored screw on the fixture, and the white jumper to the silver-colored screw. Connect both ground wires to a jumper *(dashed line)*, then fasten the jumper to a ground screw in the box.

Before installing a new outlet box, cable must be run from an existing box or the service panel, around or through the structural framework of studs and joists to the new outlet's position. Choose a path calling for the least labor and causing the smallest amount of damage to wall and ceiling.

An Advantageous Route: In unfinished basements or attics, you can fasten new electrical boxes directly to exposed studs or joists *(box, page 64).* In a finished room, however, you must cut openings in the wall or ceiling *(below and opposite),* or install surface wiring *(page 61).* Whenever possible, run the cable through an unfinished basement or attic, where studs and joists are exposed or readily accessible *(pages 58-59).* You can either staple the cable along studs and joists, or drill holes and thread the cable through them.

When tapping a wall box in a finished room just above the basement or below the attic, you can reach the box by drilling through the boards, called plates, at the top or bottom of the wall. Fish tapes—hooked wires—are then used to pull the cable along this part of its course.

Opening Hidden Paths: To run cable in a finished room that cannot be reached from basement or attic, you must make access holes in walls or ceilings to get at studs, joists, and plates along the intended route *(page 60).* Wherever the room's wooden framework blocks the way, you will have to bore a path. Fish tapes are used to guide the cable through the hidden spaces and boreholes.

Code Requirements: Cable running along an exposed joist or stud must be stapled at intervals no greater than $4\frac{1}{2}$ feet. Holes for threading cable must be drilled at least $1\frac{1}{2}$ inches from the edge of a stud or joist. Exposed cable must be stapled within 12 inches of a metal box or plastic box with an internal clamp, and 8 inches from a plastic box with no internal clamp.

 Before beginning any of these tasks, turn off power to the work area and check that all circuits on both sides of the wall are off (pages 52-53).

 TOOLS

Voltage tester	Hammer
Electric drill	Fish tapes
Spade bits	Cable ripper
($\frac{3}{8}$", $\frac{3}{4}$")	Wire stripper
Wallboard	Electronic
saw	stud finder
Screwdriver	Utility knife

MATERIALS

Hanger wire	Electrician's
Outlet box	tape
Cable	Lightweight
Cable staples	chain

SAFETY TIPS

Wear goggles when operating a power tool.

CUTTING A WALL-BOX OPENING

1. Outlining the box on the wall.

◆ Place the box face down on a sheet of thick paper and outline the box on the paper. Leave out the ears at the top and the bottom of a metal box *(right),* or at each corner of a plastic box. Mark an X within the shape, then cut out the shape. This will serve as a template.

◆ With the marked side against the wall, hold the template where you want the box, then transfer its shape to the wall.

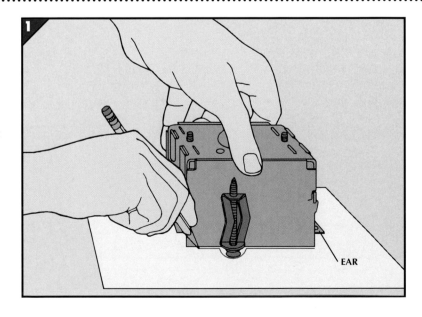

EAR

2. Cutting the opening.

◆ Turn off power to the work area and check that all circuits are off *(pages 52-53)*.

◆ Drill a small hole in the center of the outline. Bend hanger wire to a 90-degree angle, insert one end through the hole, and rotate the wire to check for obstructions. If you find any, relocate the box.

◆ With a $\frac{3}{8}$-inch spade bit, drill eight holes, positioned around the box outline *(right)*. Omit the side holes for metal boxes without clamps and for plastic boxes.

◆ Cut around the outline with a wallboard saw *(photograph)*, being careful not to cut into any wires. Use short strokes in order to avoid jabbing the saw blade into the other side of the wall.

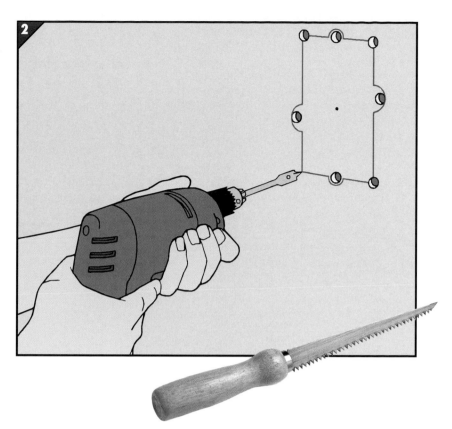

MAKING A HOLE FOR A CEILING BOX

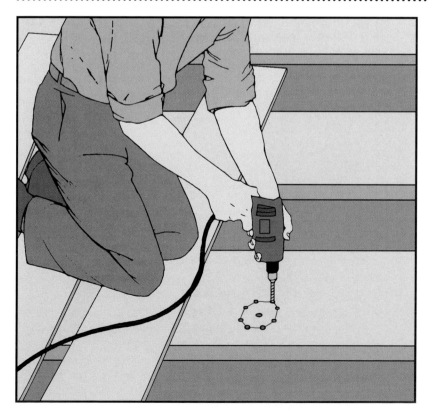

Cutting the opening.

◆ Turn off power to the work area and check that all circuits are off *(pages 52-53)*.

◆ From the room below, use an electronic stud finder to choose a location for the new box that is at least 4 inches from a joist. Mark the spot on the ceiling and drill a $\frac{1}{8}$-inch locator hole through the ceiling.

◆ In the attic, check that no wires will obstruct the new box, then center the box over the locator hole and trace the box outline on the exposed surface of the ceiling below.

◆ Drill $\frac{3}{8}$-inch holes at the outline's eight corners, positioning the bit just outside each corner *(left)*.

◆ From below, cut along the outline marked by the drilled holes with a wallboard saw.

1. Accessing an existing box.

◆ Turn off power to the work area and check that all circuits on both sides of the wall are turned off *(pages 52-53)*.

◆ Bore a $\frac{1}{8}$-inch location hole through the floor directly below the front of the box you plan to tap.

◆ Poke a thin wire or other marker through the hole, then go to the basement and find the marker.

◆ In line with the location hole, bore up through the soleplate of the wall with a $\frac{3}{4}$-inch spade bit, drilling at a slight angle if necessary *(right)*.

◆ Below the opening for the new box *(pages 56-57)*, drill a hole through the plate.

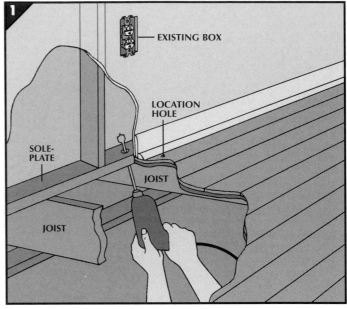

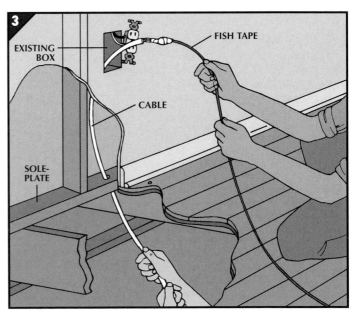

2. Fishing tape from box to basement.

◆ Detach the receptacle from the existing box and pull it out of the way; you need not disconnect the wires.

◆ With a screwdriver, remove a knockout from a hole in the bottom of the box *(page 63, Step 1)*.

◆ Push the end of a fish tape through this hole and down behind the wall.

◆ Have a helper in the basement push a fish tape up through the hole in the soleplate. Maneuver them behind the wall to hook their ends together *(left)*.

3. Feeding cable to the existing box.

◆ From the basement, pull the fish tapes that have been joined through the soleplate until the end of the upper one is exposed; unhook the tapes.

◆ With a cable ripper, strip 3 inches of sheathing from one end of the cable, then remove the insulation from the exposed wires using a wire stripper. Run the bare wires through the hook of the upper tape, then fold the wires back over themselves to secure them to the hook. Fasten the looped wires together with electrician's tape.

◆ As your helper feeds cable up through the hole in the soleplate, pull the fish tape back through the knockout hole in the existing box until the end of the cable emerges.

◆ Detach the cable from the fish tape and trim the uninsulated wires from the cable.

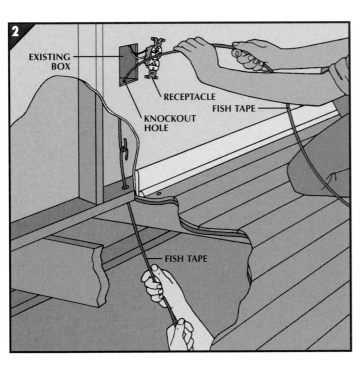

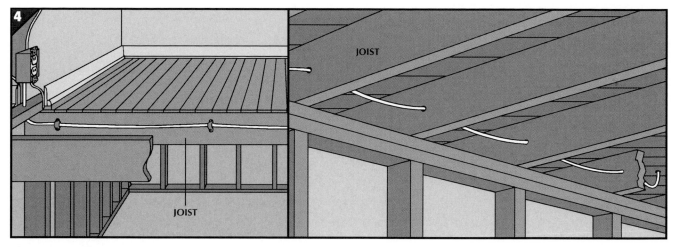

4. Running the cable.

◆ To run the cable along a joist, fasten it with cable staples *(above, left)*, taking care not to damage the cable sheathing as you nail the staples.

If you must cross joists, drill a $\frac{3}{4}$-inch hole through the middle of each joist, aligning the holes, and thread the cable through them *(above, right)*.

◆ When you reach the hole you have drilled in the opposite sole-plate, fish the cable up to the new box opening by the method shown in Steps 2 and 3.

ROUTING CABLE THROUGH AN ATTIC

Fishing cable to the attic.
You can run cable along or across exposed attic joists by the same methods used in the basement, but a light chain used in place of one fish tape simplifies the procedure.

◆ Remove a knockout from a hole in the top of the existing box *(page 63, Step 1)*.

◆ Bore a location hole in the ceiling directly above the front of the box *(opposite, Step 1)*. Then go to the attic and drill a hole through the wall's top plates in line with the location hole.

◆ Return to the room and have a helper in the attic drop a light chain down through the hole in the top plates to a point that is below the level of the box.

◆ Push a fish tape through the knockout hole, catch the chain *(right)*, and pull it into the box. Secure the chain to the hook at the end of the fish tape with electrician's tape.

◆ Have your partner pull the chain up until the fish tape reaches the attic. Remove the chain and attach the cable to the tape hook.

◆ From the room, pull the fish tape down until the end of the cable emerges in the existing box.

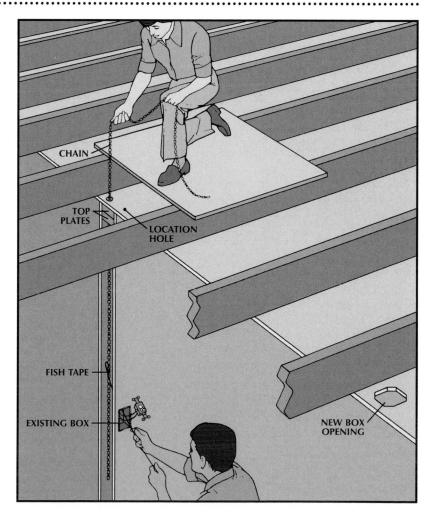

RUNNING CABLE WITHIN A WALL

1. Exposing the studs.

◆ Make an opening for the new box *(pages 56-57)*.
◆ With a stud finder, locate the stud nearest the existing box. Use a utility knife or wallboard saw to cut a hole 3 inches high and wide enough to extend 2 inches beyond the edges of the stud *(above)*.
◆ Locate the remaining studs and cut holes over them by the same method.
◆ Drill a $\frac{3}{4}$-inch hole at the center of each stud, angling the holes slightly as necessary.

2. Threading cable through the studs.

◆ After removing a knockout tab in the bottom of the existing box, have a helper push a fish tape through the hole and down into the wall.
◆ Thread a second tape through the hole in the nearest stud, hook your helper's tape *(above)*, and pull it through the stud.
◆ Release your tape, attach cable to the free end of the first tape, then have your helper pull tape and cable back through the stud and into the existing box.
◆ Using the same two-tape method, fish the other end of the cable through each stud and into the opening for the new box.

Cutting into finished walls to install new receptacles can be a daunting task. If you have a minimal amount of rewiring to do, this can be avoided in a number of ways: by installing surface-mounted conduit, multi-outlet strips, power bars, or a receptacle adapter. All these methods can help avoid an unsightly and potentially dangerous mess of extension cords, although the wires will be visible. Whatever method you choose, be sure that the equipment you plan to plug in won't overload the existing circuit *(page 48).*

Surface-Mounted Conduit: A system of channels and outlet boxes, surface-mounted conduit is installed along baseboards, door-frames, and the ceiling *(below)*; the rigid

channels that protect the wires all but vanish when painted to match the room. Follow the manufacturer's instructions for installation.

Multiplying Outlets: If you require new outlets primarily along one wall, you can add them without running new cable. One way is to install a multi-outlet strip, which is direct-wired to the circuit *(page 62).* An easy, but less permanent-looking alternative is to simply purchase a power bar or receptacle adapter *(box, page 62).*

⚠ **CAUTION** *Before installing surface raceways or a multi-outlet strip, turn off power to the affected circuits and check that it is off on both sides of the wall* (pages 52-53).

TOOLS

Screwdriver
Cable ripper
Wire stripper

MATERIALS

Raceway channel
  and fittings
Multi-outlet strip
Electrical cable
Wire caps

RACEWAYS FOR WALLS AND CEILINGS

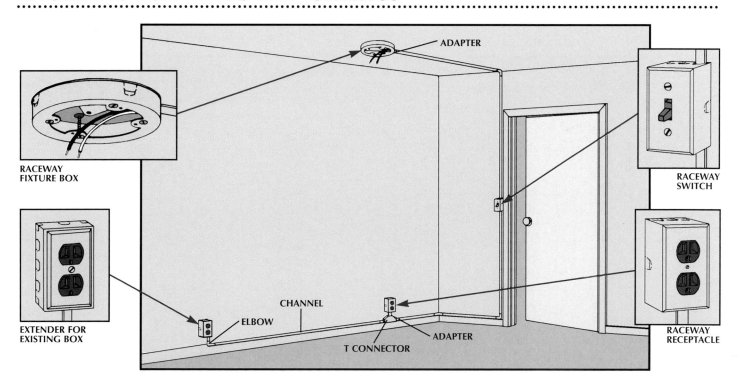

RACEWAY FIXTURE BOX

EXTENDER FOR EXISTING BOX

ELBOW · **CHANNEL** · **T CONNECTOR** · **ADAPTER**

ADAPTER

RACEWAY SWITCH

RACEWAY RECEPTACLE

A network of raceway fittings.
Raceway elements are available in both metal and plastic. Fittings like boxes and elbows come in two pieces: a backplate that screws to the wall and a cover, which snaps over the plate. The backplate of each fitting has tongues

that slip into the ends of the single-piece channel; the width of channel to use depends on the number and gauge of the wires in the circuit. Metal raceway systems accommodate cable, but individual wires labeled type TW on the insulation are easier to install.

Only hot and neutral wires are needed; the channel itself, along with wires inside each outlet box, takes care of grounding. Plastic systems, however, require running a ground wire alongside the black and white ones and connecting it to each fixture in the circuit.

Mounting the strip.

◆ Mark the desired location of the multi-outlet strip, indicating the position of the small junction box.

◆ Run cable to the junction-box location.

◆ Separate the base from the strip and screw it to the wall *(right)*.

◆ Cut the sheathing from the end of the cable with a cable ripper and strip the ends of the wires using a wire stripper.

◆ With wire caps, connect the bare cable wire to the green wire of the outlet strip; the white cable wire to the white outlet wire; and the black cable wire to the black outlet wire.

◆ At the other end of the strip, connect the green wire to the grounding clip that clamps into the outlet-strip base. Cover exposed wire ends with wire caps.

◆ Snap the outlet strip onto the base.

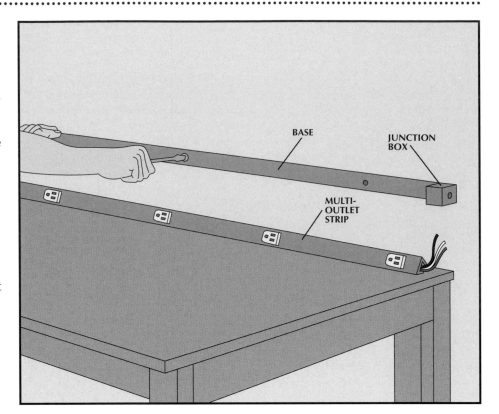

BASE

JUNCTION BOX

MULTI-OUTLET STRIP

POWER BARS AND RECEPTACLE ADAPTERS

The simplest way to accommodate new equipment is to use a power bar or a receptacle adapter. Power bars sit on the floor or can be fastened to a desk or wall, serving as extensions and additional receptacles. Receptacle adapters simply increase the number of slots at a receptacle. The model shown has slots on the side so it occupies less space between the back of a desk and the wall. Many power bars and receptacle adapters include a built-in circuit breaker; for sensitive computer equipment, choose one with a surge-suppression feature.

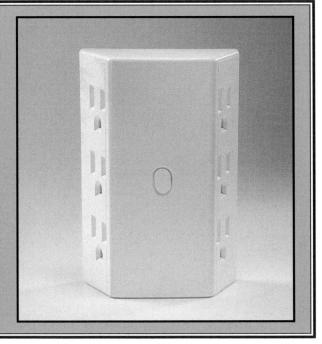

The central element in any electrical installation is an outlet box mounted in a wall or ceiling. The box supports switches, receptacles, and light fixtures, and protects connections to the house wiring.

Installing the Boxes: Outlet boxes that house receptacles, switches, and wall lights are generally rectangular. They can be made either of metal or plastic. In finished walls, they are clamped to the wallboard, while in an unfinished room, they can be attached directly to the studs *(below and page 64)*.

Boxes for ceiling lights are octagonal or circular. To support most ceiling fixtures, the box must be metal and be firmly fastened to two joists. One type is fastened to joists from an unfinished attic *(page 65)*, while another type can be installed from below when the area above is inaccessible *(box, page 66)*. To support a ceiling fan, use only boxes approved for that purpose. Before installing an outlet box, clamp the wire securely to the box; the method differs depending on the type of box.

Connecting the Wires: Once the box is in place, the receptacle or switch can be hooked up. When you buy a new receptacle, make sure it is rated for the correct voltage and amperage—and that it can be grounded. The way the receptacle is hooked up to the cable depends on whether it is located in the middle or at the end of the circuit *(page 66)*.

The function of a switch is to interrupt a hot wire in a circuit. As with receptacles, the wiring method for a switch depends on its location in the circuit *(page 67)*. One common arrangement is a middle-of-the-run switch—where the current encounters the switch before the fixture. A switch loop is used where cable runs to a light before it reaches the switch.

Once the receptacle or switch is hooked up, connect the other end of the cable to the old outlet box *(page 55)* or, for a new circuit, have an electrician connect it to the service panel. Finally, check your work *(pages 52-53)*.

 TOOLS

Screwdriver	Tin snips	Nail set
Pliers	Electric drill	Cable ripper
Wallboard saw	Hammer	Wire stripper

 **MATERIALS**

Wall box	Two-part	Receptacles
Ceiling box	connectors	Jumper wires
Cable	Bar hanger	Wire caps

INSTALLING A METAL WALL BOX

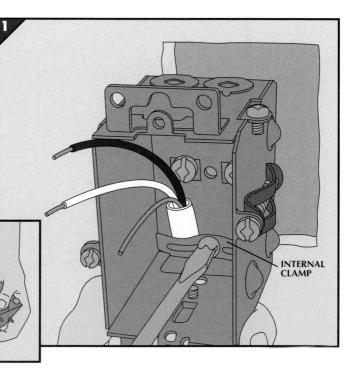

1. Clamping the cable.
◆ Insert the tip of a screwdriver into the slot of a U-shaped knockout, and pry the knockout away from the box *(inset)*.
◆ Work the knockout back and forth until it breaks free; if necessary, twist it out with pliers.
◆ With a cable ripper, cut 3 inches of sheathing from the end of the cable, then strip the ends of the wires with wire strippers. Pull the cable into the box through the knockout hole and under the internal clamp, leaving 6 inches of cable extending past the front of the box.
◆ Holding the cable so the clamp rests on the sheathed portion, screw the clamp tightly against the cable *(right)*.

INTERNAL CLAMP

2. Setting the box in the wall.

◆ Check for fit by pushing the box into the wall opening. Remove the box, enlarge the hole as necessary with a wallboard saw, and move the ears by turning the adjustment screw to bring the box flush with the wall.

◆ Return the box to the opening. Tighten the clamp screws on the sides, expanding the clamps and drawing the box against the wall *(right)*.

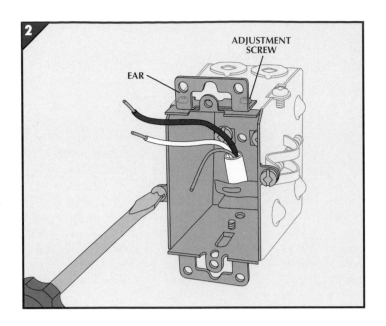

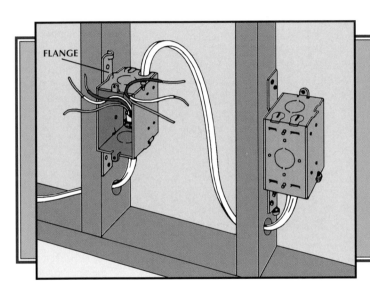

BOXES FOR AN UNFINISHED ROOM

In an unfinished room, rough in the wiring before putting up the wallboard. Nail flanged outlet boxes to the studs so the edge of the flange is flush with the edge of the stud. Drill $\frac{3}{4}$-inch holes through the studs near the soleplate and run the cable, clamping it securely to each box. Avoid placing outlet boxes that serve adjacent rooms within the same stud space; doing so will conduct sound between the rooms. Staple the cable to the studs.

A PLASTIC BOX

Attaching the box.

◆ With a wallboard saw or a drill, enlarge the holes in the upper right and lower left corners of the opening to accommodate the clamps.

◆ Press firmly on the clamp from the rear of the box with your finger or a screwdriver to break the thin plastic locking it closed.

◆ Cut the sheathing from the cable with a cable ripper, then strip the ends of the wires with a wire stripper.

◆ From outside the box, push the wires under the flap, then pull the cable into the box. Press the clamp against the cable sheathing to ensure a good grip.

◆ Insert the box into the opening.

◆ Tighten the screws on the top right and bottom left corners of the box *(right)*. Doing so extends the clamps and draws them toward the inside of the wall, pulling the box tight.

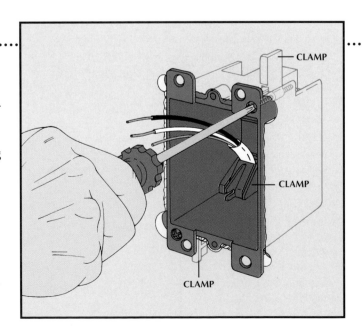

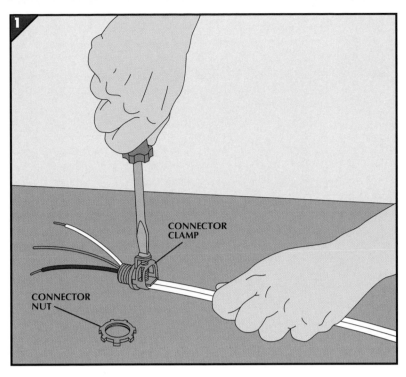

1. Clamping the cable.

◆ Remove a round knockout from the side of the box with a hammer and nail set.

◆ Cut the sheathing from the end of the cable with a cable ripper, then use wire strippers to strip the ends of the wires.

◆ Slip the clamp portion of a two-part connector onto the cable, with the threaded portion facing the stripped wires and flush with the end of the sheathing. Tighten the clamp screw on the cable *(left)*.

Some ceiling boxes have an internal clamp; in this case, clamp the cable as for a wall box *(page 63, Step 1)*.

2. Installing the box.

◆ Insert the stripped wires and the threaded end of the connector into the box through the knockout hole. Slip the nut over the wires and screw it onto the connector so it is finger tight.

◆ Fasten the box to the hanger with the hardware provided.

◆ Cut the tab from each end of an extendable bar hanger with tin snips.

◆ Holding the box in the ceiling hole with its front flush against the inside surface of the ceiling, extend the arms of the hanger to the joists on either side. Mark the positions of the hanger screw holes on the joists, drill pilot holes, and screw the hanger to the joists *(right)*.

◆ From below, position a nail set against one of the protrusions on the rim of the connector nut; tap the nail set, tightening the nut *(inset)*.

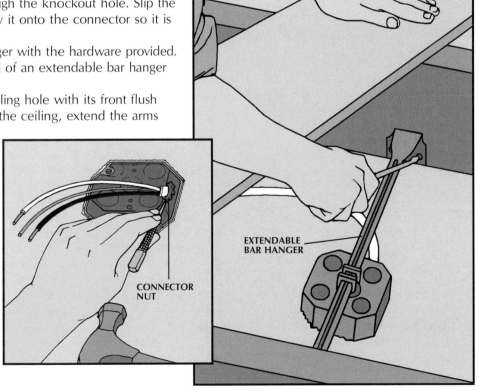

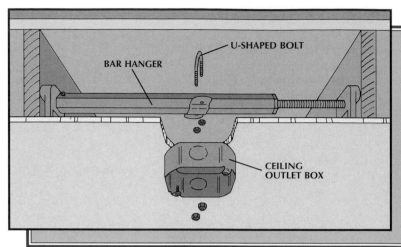

BAR HANGER

U-SHAPED BOLT

CEILING OUTLET BOX

A screw-type bar hanger is designed to be installed from below when the joists are not accessible from an unfinished attic above. The bar hanger is inserted into the hole in the ceiling and turned by hand to extend the ends to reach the joists. An adjustable wrench is used to turn the bar, forcing the teeth on each end into the joists. Once the bar is in place, the ceiling outlet box is attached to it with the U-shaped bolt and nuts provided.

WIRING A RECEPTACLE

Middle-of-the-run

Two cables enter a box in the middle of a circuit run, each containing black, white, and bare copper wires.

◆ Connect each black wire to a brass-colored terminal in any order.

◆ Attach the white wires to the silver-colored terminals.

◆ In a metal box, attach a short jumper to the back of the box with a machine screw and attach another jumper to the green grounding terminal on the receptacle.

◆ Fasten these jumpers and the two bare copper wires from the cables with a wire cap *(right)*. For a plastic box, there will be no jumper needed to the box.

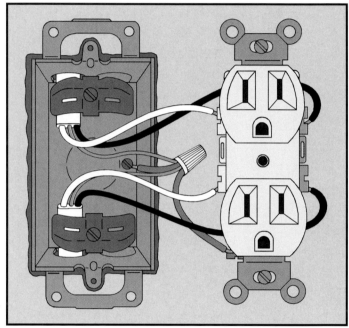

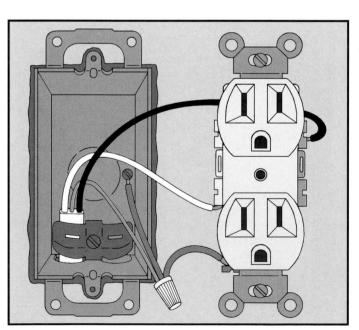

End-of-the-run.

Only one cable enters an end-of-the-run box.

◆ With plastic-sheathed cable, connect the one black wire to either brass-colored terminal and the white wire to either silver terminal.

◆ With a metal box, attach ground jumpers to the box and receptacle, and connect them to the bare copper wire with a wire cap. With a plastic box, there is no jumper to the box.

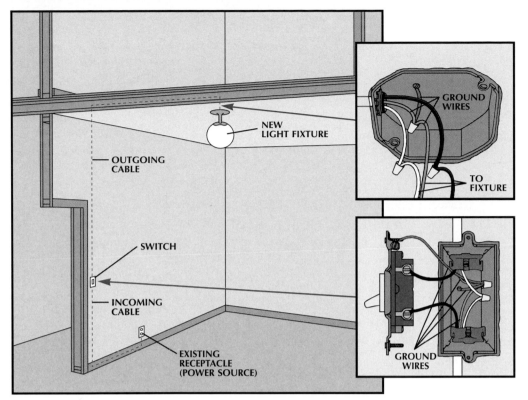

A middle-of-the-run switch.

◆ At the switch *(bottom inset)*, attach the black wires of the incoming and outgoing cables to the switch, join the white wires with a wire cap, and screw a ground wire to the box—if it is metal.

◆ Connect the black and white fixture wires to their counterparts in the cable *(top inset)*. Do likewise with the ground wires, adding a jumper to the box if it is metal.

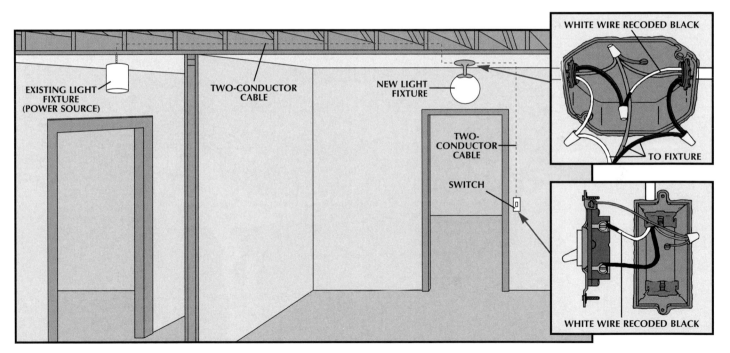

A switch loop.

◆ At the new fixture *(top inset)*, join the incoming white wire to the white fixture wire. Blacken the end of the white wire of the outgoing, switch-loop cable to show that the wire is hot and connect it to the black wire of the incoming cable. Attach the black fixture wire to the black wire in the switch loop. Join the ground wires and connect them to the box, if it is metal, with a jumper.

◆ At the switch *(bottom inset)*, recode the white wire black, and connect both conductors to the switch. Connect the ground wire with jumpers to the switch and to the box—if it is metal.

Installing New Light Fixtures

The most suitable ceiling fixtures for a home office are standard suspended fixtures, recessed fixtures, and fluorescent lights. Suspended fixtures and fluorescents are hooked up to a ceiling box—to support any fixture heavier than 5 pounds, ensure that the box is metal and is securely fastened to the joists *(pages 65-66)*. Most fixtures come with their own mounting hardware, and the recessed type—both halogen and standard incandescent—include their own wiring box.

Suspended Fixtures: The most common type of fixture, suspended incandescent lights, can sometimes be attached directly to the mounting tabs in the ceiling box. In other cases, you will have to adapt the box with a crossbar *(below)*.

Recessed Lights: Standard incandescent fixtures hang from a mounting plate inserted into the ceiling opening and sit flush with the ceiling *(opposite and page 70)*. When installing several such units on a single circuit, make sure that all but one are rated for "through-wiring" with two cables; the last fixture needs only a single cable. Halogen fixtures are unusual in that as well as a built-in wiring box, they incorporate a transformer to convert the house current to the lower voltage needed by a halogen bulb *(pages 71-72)*.

Fluorescent Lights: Available in a number of shapes, the most common fluorescent fixture is the rectangular one-tube model *(page 72)*. Circular fixtures are also available.

 CAUTION Before installing a light fixture, turn off all the circuits in the work area and make sure they are off. When you have finished the job, check your work (pages 52-53).

 **TOOLS**
	Electronic
	stud finder
Fish tape	Electric drill
Cable ripper	Spade bits
Wire stripper	($\frac{5}{8}$", $\frac{3}{4}$")
Screwdriver	Wallboard
Hacksaw	saw
Tin snips	Hammer

MATERIALS
Light fixture kit	Wallboard
Cable	patching
Jumper wire	materials
Wire caps	Toggle bolts,
Crossbar	washers
Lock nut	Hickey
Two-part	Nipple
connector	

 SAFETY TIPS

Wear goggles when sawing or drilling.

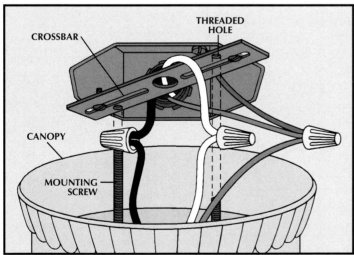

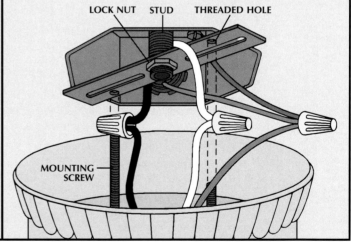

A suspended fixture.
◆ Fish a cable to the ceiling box, clamp it, remove the insulation from the end of the cable, and strip the wires.
◆ With wire caps, connect black wires to black, and white wires to white. In a metal box, fasten a short jumper to the box with a machine screw, then connect the jumper and the bare copper wires with a wire cap. (For a plastic box no jumper to the box is needed.)

◆ Where canopy holes do not align with the mounting tabs in the ceiling box, adapt the box with a slotted crossbar. Screw the crossbar to the tabs *(above, left),* or for a box with a stud in the center, slip the crossbar onto the stud and secure it with a lock nut *(above, right).*
◆ Fasten the canopy to the threaded holes in the crossbar with screws trimmed, if necessary, so they do not press against the back of the box.

INSTALLING A STANDARD RECESSED FIXTURE

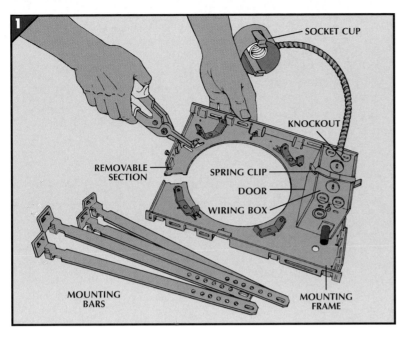

1. Preparing the mounting frame.

◆ If a template is not provided with the fixture, create one by removing the frame's mounting bars and placing the frame on a piece of cardboard. Outline the frame and circular opening with a pencil, then cut along the lines to create a template.

◆ With tin snips, cut out the removable section of the frame opposite the wiring box *(left)*.

◆ Lift the spring clip on top of the wiring box and remove one of its two detachable doors.

2. Cutting a ceiling opening.

◆ With an electronic stud finder, locate the ceiling joists. Using the template, mark fixture locations on the ceiling between joists.

◆ Drill a small hole in the center of each circular mark. Bend hanger wire to a 90-degree angle, insert one end through the hole, and rotate the wire to check for obstructions. If you find any, relocate the fixtures. Otherwise, cut openings as shown on page 57.

◆ At each joist running between fixtures, cut an access opening in the ceiling as shown for studs on page 60. Drill a $\frac{3}{4}$-inch hole through the center of each joist.

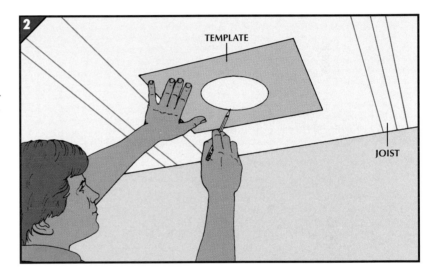

3. Wiring connections.

◆ Fish a cable from a junction box to the first fixture opening, followed by another cable from the second fixture opening to the first—and so on downstream. Remove insulation from the ends of the cables and strip the wires.

◆ At the first ceiling opening, rest a fixture-mounting frame atop a stepladder, and clamp the cable ends to opposite sides of the box.

◆ Red wire caps *(left)* indicate the connections to be made between the cable and fixture wires. Connect black to black, white to white, and the ground wires.

◆ Reattach the box door.

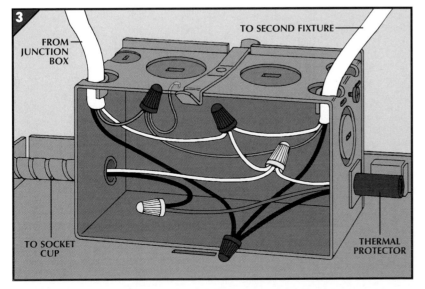

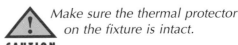

⚠ **CAUTION** *Make sure the thermal protector on the fixture is intact.*

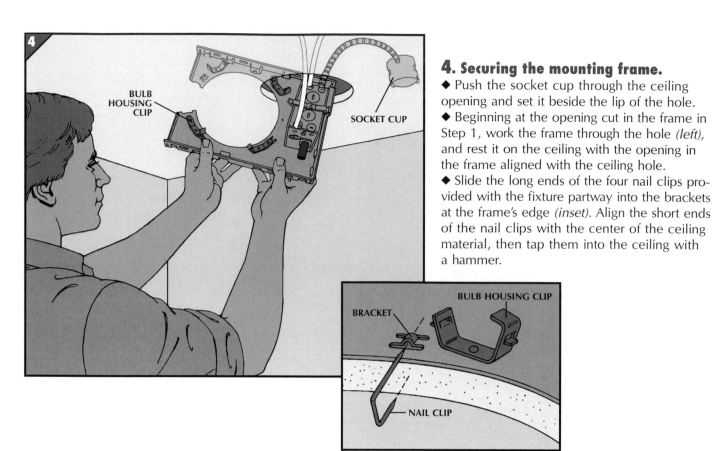

4. Securing the mounting frame.

◆ Push the socket cup through the ceiling opening and set it beside the lip of the hole.

◆ Beginning at the opening cut in the frame in Step 1, work the frame through the hole *(left),* and rest it on the ceiling with the opening in the frame aligned with the ceiling hole.

◆ Slide the long ends of the four nail clips provided with the fixture partway into the brackets at the frame's edge *(inset).* Align the short ends of the nail clips with the center of the ceiling material, then tap them into the ceiling with a hammer.

5. Installing the bulb housing.

◆ Bring the socket cup back through the opening. Rotate the bulb housing clips inward.

◆ Insert the socket cup into the top of the bulb housing so that tabs in the cup snap into slots in the housing.

◆ Push the assembly into the frame *(right)* until the bulb housing flange rests against the ceiling, completing the installation.

◆ At the second fixture opening, connect cables from the first and third fixture openings to the second fixture in its wiring box, and complete the installation as described above.

◆ When all fixtures are in place, patch the access holes at each joist.

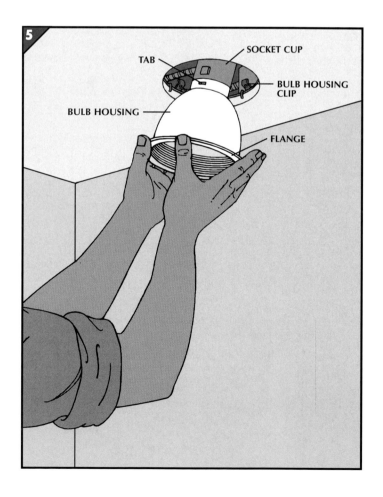

A RECESSED HALOGEN LIGHT

1. Making the wiring connections.

◆ Using the template provided, cut a hole in the ceiling *(page 69, Step 2)*. Route cable to the opening.

◆ Remove the insulation from the end of the cable and strip the wires.

◆ Set the fixture on a ladder near the opening. Remove the cover from the junction box. Then, remove a knockout and clamp the cable to the box with a two-part connector *(page 65, Step 1)*.

◆ Red wire caps indicate the cable and fixture wires to be connected: the black wire to the black, the green wire to the the copper ground wire, and the white wire to the white *(right)*.

◆ Push the wires into the box and replace the cover.

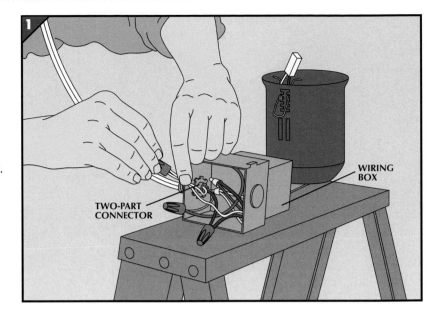

TWO-PART CONNECTOR

WIRING BOX

2. Installing the fixture.

◆ Lift the fixture into the opening with the wiring box first *(left)*, then center the housing over the opening.

◆ Reaching inside the housing, push up on the metal prongs to press the springs down against the wallboard, then clip the prongs into the slots in the housing *(inset)*. If the spring is overly tight, remove it and reattach it to a higher pair of tabs. If it is too loose, attach it to a lower pair of tabs.

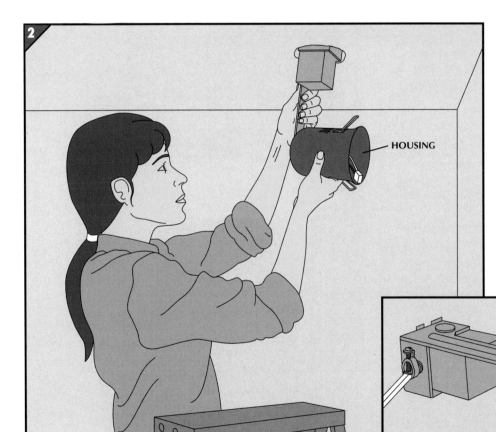

HOUSING

SLOT

PRONG

TAB

SPRING

HOUSING

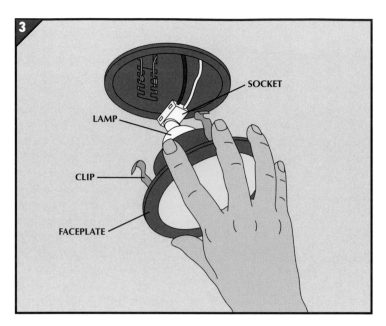

3. Attaching the lamp.
◆ Remove the cardboard covering the glass lens of the faceplate and slip the lamp into place.
◆ Insert the prongs on the end of the lamp into the socket hanging from the wires inside the housing.
◆ Push the faceplate up into the housing until it is snug against the ceiling.

A FLUORESCENT FIXTURE

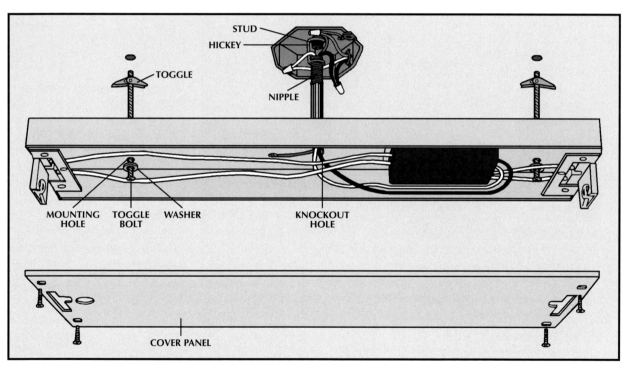

Mounting a one-tube ceiling fixture.
◆ Position the fixture with the knockout hole for the wires centered on the ceiling box, and mark the ceiling through the fixture-mounting holes. Lower the fixture and, with a $\frac{5}{8}$-inch spade bit, drill holes at the marks.
◆ Slip a toggle bolt and washer through the fixture-mounting holes and screw a toggle onto the end of each of the bolts.
◆ Thread a hickey to the stud and a nipple to the hickey; if there is no stud, attach a crossbar (*page 68*) to the box tabs and a nipple to the crossbar.

◆ Have a helper support the fixture or hang it from the box with a wire hanger, then lead the fixture wires through the nipple and connect them to those that are in the box, black to black and white to white. Connect the ground wires from the fixture and the house circuit to each other and to the grounding jumper in the box if it is metal.
◆ Raise the fixture. While folding the wires into the box, push the toggles through the ceiling holes and guide the fixture onto the nipple. Tighten the toggle bolts.
◆ Finally, install the cover panel and the tube.

A home office will require one or more jacks for fax and modem connections. You most likely will also want to install independent phone lines in the office.

A typical home telephone system is linked to the network by a special jack or by a box called a network interface. The device serves as a point of demarcation between the phone company's jurisdiction and the homeowner's. This link and everything beyond it is installed and maintained by the phone company, but anywhere on your home's side of the boundary, you are free to modify and expand the system. Within the house, jacks are wired either to each other or to a central connecting block, usually located in a basement, attic, or utility room.

Adding New Jacks: Phone jacks can be mounted on a baseboard or set into the wall like an electrical receptacle *(page 74)*. To merely extend a line, it's easiest to wire new jacks to a nearby jack on an existing phone line; locate them at least 6 inches from the nearest electrical outlet.

Adding New Lines: Every independent phone line serving a home requires a pair of wires—two pairs are usually provided by the phone company so that two separate phone lines can be accommodated. To add more lines, the phone company will need to bring in additional wires.

To hook up a second line, you can reconfigure an existing jack *(box, page 74)*, purchase a two-line telephone, or install a special two-line jack. Alternatively, route cable called telephone station wire from each jack serving the new line directly to the point of demarcation, and have the phone company make the connection there. This allows for greater flexibility later on, since any of these jacks can be switched to a new line simply by changing the connections at the point of demarcation. If you are installing new jacks with home-run wiring, consider using three-pair twisted wire *(below)* to permit future upgrades.

Running Cable: Telephone station wire can be run inside walls and through unfinished attics and basements much as electrical cable can *(pages 58-60)*, as long as it is kept 6 inches from electrical wiring. However, since it carries such low voltage, it can also be run along baseboards *(page 75)* and around door and window frames, or you can hide it behind shoe molding or under the edge of wall-to-wall carpet. To bring station wire from one floor to another, you can route it through closets or take advantage of the open space around a plumbing stack vent *(page 76)*.

> ⚠️ **CAUTION** Although the message-carrying current in a phone line is harmless, the phone is rung by bursts of current strong enough to deliver a mild shock. To prevent phones from ringing while you are working with wires, remove all phone handsets from the hooks.

 TOOLS

Screwdriver
Wire strippers
Diagonal cutters
Staple gun for attaching wires
Electric drill
Fish tapes
Fishing weight

 **MATERIALS**

Telephone jacks
Telephone station wire
Wire clips
Telephone-wire staples
Heavy string

 SAFETY TIPS

When drilling, protect your eyes with goggles.

OPTIONS IN TELEPHONE WIRE

Older homes usually have telephone wires that carry quad wire—two pairs of untwisted wires, with each pair designed to serve a separate telephone number. When both lines are in use with this type of wire, you can experience "crosstalk" between the two lines. While crosstalk may be merely annoying when you are speaking on a phone, on a modem or fax line it can disrupt transmission of data. If you are installing new runs of telephone wire, consider buying three-pair twisted wire. Twisted wire prevents crosstalk; the three-pair type can accommodate a third line.

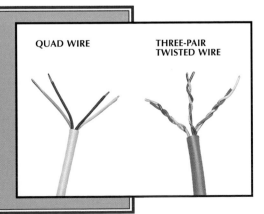

QUAD WIRE   THREE-PAIR TWISTED WIRE

INSTALLING TELEPHONE JACKS

Putting in a surface-mounted jack.
◆ Loosen the four terminal screws on the jack about three turns each.
◆ Remove 3 inches of sheathing from a length of telephone station wire to reveal the colored conductors.
◆ Insert each colored wire into the slot of its corresponding color-coded terminal *(right)*.
◆ Attach the jack to the baseboard with the screws provided.
◆ Insert the spade tips on the jack-cover wires into their corresponding color-coded terminals and tighten the screws.
◆ Break out a wire-channel tab from the jack cover, route the station wire through it, and then screw the cover to the jack.
◆ Route the station wire to an active jack, securing it with wire clips, and connect the conductors to the appropriate color-coded terminals there.

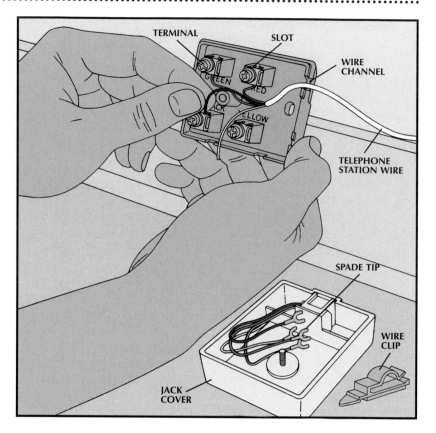

Installing a flush-mounted jack.
◆ Install a standard electrical outlet box *(pages 63-64)* and route a length of telephone station wire from an active jack into the box.
◆ Remove 3 inches of sheathing from the station wire and $\frac{1}{2}$ inch of insulation from each colored conductor.
◆ Loosen the four terminal screws about three turns.
◆ Wrap the bare end of each conductor around a terminal, matching the color of the wire already installed there *(left)*. Tighten the screws.
◆ Trim stray wire ends with diagonal cutters, and attach the jack to the outlet box with the screws provided.

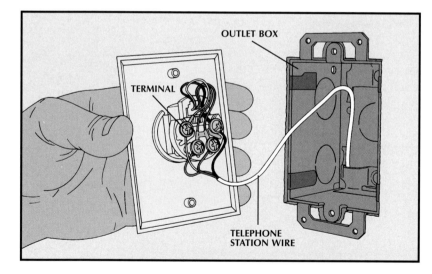

WHICH PHONE RINGS WHERE

Jacks installed by the telephone company are always wired to serve two lines. To reconfigure a surface-mounted jack to serve only the second line, open the jack and remove the red and green spade tips from the terminals. Wrap the tips with electrical tape and fold them out of the way. Leave all the colored conductors from the telephone station wire connected to the terminals; they supply jacks farther down the lines.

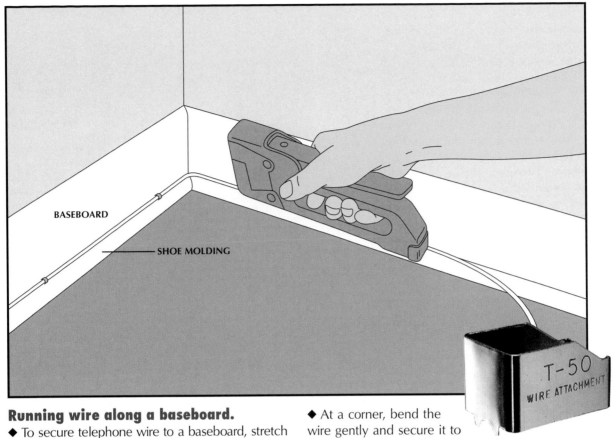

BASEBOARD

— **SHOE MOLDING**

Running wire along a baseboard.
◆ To secure telephone wire to a baseboard, stretch it along the baseboard above the shoe molding and staple it in place every 16 inches with a staple gun designed for telephone-wire staples. Some standard staple guns can be fitted with a special attachment for this purpose *(photograph)*.

◆ At a corner, bend the wire gently and secure it to each wall 2 inches from the bend *(above)*.

An alternative method is to staple the wire to the wallboard just above the baseboard.

TRICKS OF THE TRADE

Pushing Phone Wire Through a Wall

To route phone wire through a hollow wall, drill straight through the wall, then insert a drinking straw through the holes *(right)*. If the straw will not exit the second hole, push a straightened coat hanger through first and then slide the straw over it. Pull out the hanger and pass the telephone wire through the straw. Then, remove the straw and patch the gaps around the wire with spackling compound.

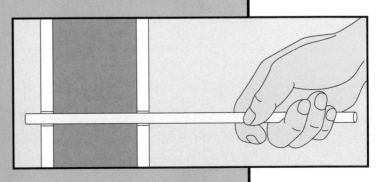

Wiring through closets.

Use the following procedure when closets are not stacked directly above one another:

◆ Fish wiring from the basement through a hole drilled in the floor of a closet above.

◆ Drill a hole through the closet ceiling into the space between the joists above *(right)*.

◆ Drill a hole down into the same joist space through the floor of a closet on the next floor.

◆ Tack one end of a heavy string to the floor of the upper closet. Wrap the other end into loops, and stuff the loops down into the joist space.

◆ Push a fish tape through the hole in the lower closet and snag the string *(inset)*. Pull the string into the lower closet, tie it to the wiring, and pull them into the upper closet.

If the closets do not share a joist space, remove a section of baseboard in an upper room and drill behind it on an angle into the joist space above the lower closet. Fish wiring through and run it along the baseboard to the nearest jack location.

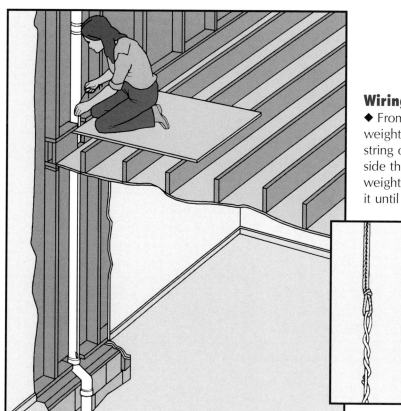

Wiring along a stack vent.

◆ From the attic, lower a small fishing weight attached to a long piece of string or chain into the space alongside the plumbing stack *(left)*. If the weight is blocked, jiggle and bounce it until it falls past the obstruction.

◆ When the string reaches the basement, attach cables to the string, staggering the points of attachment to avoid a bulky connection *(inset)*.

◆ Pull the string and cables back up beside the stack.

Once you've found a corner of the house for your office where you'll be undisturbed, you may still need to communicate with family members in other rooms or a visitor who comes to the front door. This is best done with an intercom, of which there are three main types: In one, units located throughout the house communicate by radio waves; in another, the units plug into electrical receptacles and communicate over the house wiring; in the third, called a hard-wired system, units are linked by low-voltage wire run through walls and along baseboards in the same way as telephone wire *(pages 75-76)*. The first two systems are easy to install and relatively inexpensive; however, for much clearer sound—free from interference—the hard-wired system wins.

In the simplest system of any type, a master unit is installed in a closet or other hidden spot, and a number of stations are each wired directly to it. Some intercoms also allow "daisy chain" wiring, in which each station is wired to the previous one, rather than to the master unit.

Stations include indoor and outdoor units that can receive and initiate a communication with the push of a button. Other systems have a "hands-free" feature, which allows the person at the receiving end to respond to a communication without pushing a button.

Most models also include special units that allow you to talk to someone at the front door, although communication cannot be initiated from the door units. In some cases, a special door chime wired to the intercom will transmit the signal to all the stations. Some systems even allow you to unlock the door remotely.

In addition to the standard indoor stations, a desktop unit in the office can be kept within easy reach. For rooms where you want the station to be less conspicuous, a small control unit installed in an accessible spot can be wired to independent speakers hidden in a corner or in the ceiling. On many models, you can hook up a cassette deck or CD player to the master station, allowing music to be transmitted to all the stations.

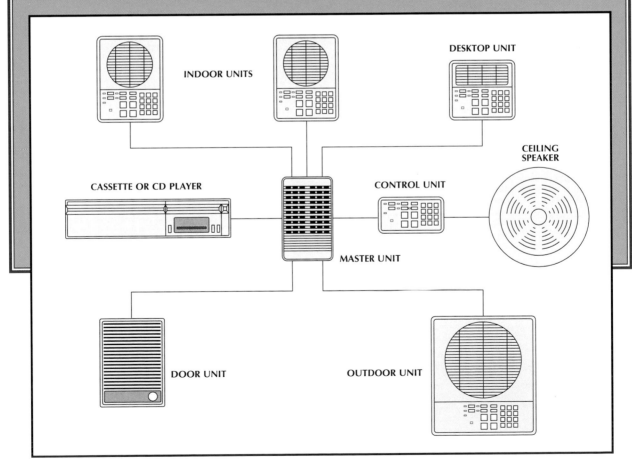

INDOOR UNITS

DESKTOP UNIT

CEILING SPEAKER

CASSETTE OR CD PLAYER

CONTROL UNIT

MASTER UNIT

DOOR UNIT

OUTDOOR UNIT

4

Furnishing Your Office

Although a wide variety of commercial office furniture is available, building your own ensures that it is both comfortable to use and suited to your particular office tasks. This chapter shows you how to contruct a custom-made workstation, a variety of storage units, and a folding desk. In addition, you'll find instructions on how to fit a compact office into a closet.

Drilling holes for shelf pegs →

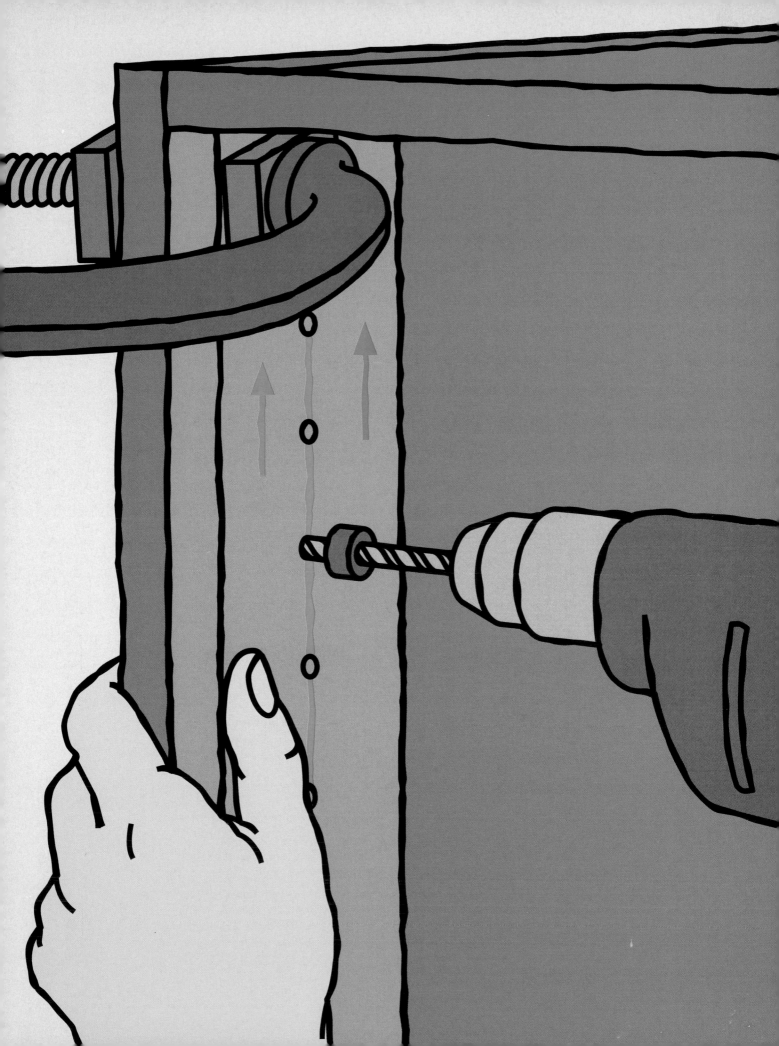

You are likely to spend more waking hours in your home office than in any other part of the house. Thus, it's important to properly plan and lay out the office and everything in it to avoid compromising your comfort and health. Designing a working environment for human comfort and safety—the science known as ergonomics—includes furnishings such as desks and chairs, and environmental factors like lighting and air quality.

Workstation Design: Much office work consists of sitting at a computer workstation. A poorly designed desk or an ill-fitting chair can contribute to back, shoulder, and neck pain; a keyboard that is incorrectly positioned can lead to repetitive stress injuries to the wrists. When building your own desk, design it so the keyboard, monitor, and documents are set at the correct height *(opposite)*. If you are buying a workstation and can't find one with the right dimensions for your size, you can compensate with adjustable supports for the monitor and keyboard. Adjust the chair to keep your arms, legs, and back at the angles shown in the diagram.

Protecting Your Eyes: To avoid eyestrain, place the monitor at the correct distance from your eyes *(opposite)*. Provide for adequate lighting *(pages 51)*. Take a break every half hour and stare off into the distance to ease the strain on your eyes.

Keeping Things Within Reach: To avoid having to stretch frequently across your desk—and perhaps strain back or shoulder muscles—set up your workstation so that the items you regularly need to use are within easy reach *(below)*. If a single work surface is not adequate, consider adding an L-shaped extension to your desk that you can reach by simply swiveling your chair.

Hearing Yourself Think: Low-level noise in your office may not be immediately noticeable, but with time it can take a toll on your concentration and efficiency. Block noise from outside the office with soundproofed walls and ceilings *(pages 38-40)*, and with carpet on the floor in the room above. Control noise originating inside the office with acoustic tiles *(page 37)*. Also, try to furnish the room so "hard" surfaces such as bare walls stand opposite "soft" ones such as bookcases or drapes. Two hard surfaces across from each other often reflect too much noise.

Breathing Easy: Vapors emitted by certain types of carpets—as well as by the toner used in photocopiers and laser printers—have been linked to respiratory disorders. The air quality in your office, particularly after installation of new carpeting, can be improved by proper ventilation. A further step to take is to filter airborne particles out of the air by installing an air purifier. Also be sure to keep your office at a comfortable temperature and humidity.

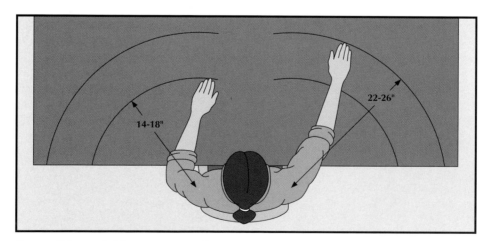

Everything within easy reach.
Position items on a desk so you can reach them without straining. The area within 14 to 18 inches of the shoulders can be reached by moving the hands only *(above)*—keep the computer mouse within this arc. Reaching the area in the 22- to 26-inch range requires extension of the arm without straining forward—ideal for documents and regularly used supplies. Reserve the area outside these arcs for seldom-used items.

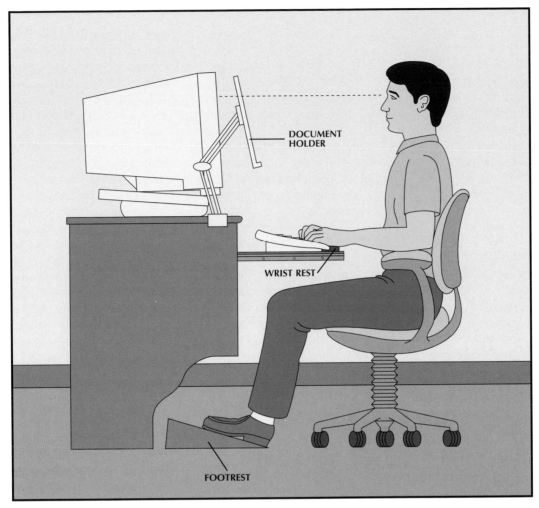

DOCUMENT HOLDER

WRIST REST

FOOTREST

Comfortable seating.

When designing your workstation *(page 82)*, observe the following guidelines: Set the chair height so the soles of your feet are flat on the floor or on a footrest, and your thighs are parallel to the floor or slope down slightly. Place the monitor 18 to 30 inches from your eyes, with the top line of the display at eye level. If you type from documents, set up a document holder close to the monitor. The keyboard must be positioned so that when your elbows are at your sides your forearms are parallel to the floor or angled slightly downward, with your wrists in line with your forearms. Position the mouse so you can reach it with your arm close to your body and with your hand and forearm in a straight line.

A padded wrist rest can help keep your wrists from bending and cushion them from a sharp desk edge, both common causes of repetitive stress injuries. Purchase a wrist rest long enough to span the length of both the keyboard and mouse area—or get a second, smaller wrist rest for the mouse alone.

A Custom Workstation

The workstations and amenities shown here and on the following pages represent only a selection of the possibilities that you can fashion from the instructions that follow in this chapter. Individual elements, each built separately, can be adapted and combined to create various setups.

You can build working surfaces to a comfortable height *(pages 80-81)*, and include as many compartments, drawers, and shelves as necessary to house equipment and meet storage needs.

The Work Surface: A standard desk is 60 inches long by 30 inches deep and 29 inches high. Because sitting at a desk this large would place many items out of reach *(page 80)*, you can include a special corner unit that joins two desks at right angles *(below and opposite)*.

A desk should be large enough to accommodate a computer; other equipment such as printers and fax machines can also go on a desk, or on shelving above it or on a separate rolling unit.

Designing for Computers: If you have a large computer monitor and your work surface won't be able to accommodate both the monitor and the keyboard, a pullout keyboard tray *(page 112)* will enable you to position the keyboard at the correct distance from the screen, and at a comfortable height. Plan the height of the keyboard tray so your forearms will be roughly parallel to the floor when you are typing; to

ensure the tray will clear your knees, you may have to mount the tray or desktop a bit higher. When the monitor and central processing unit (CPU) are separate components, the monitor may fit on top of a CPU in a horizontal housing; take care that the monitor isn't too high for comfort *(page 81)*. A vertical CPU can rest on the floor or in a special compartment built into a work-surface support.

Storage Space: In addition to the cabinets supporting the work surface, you can add storage space by placing a shelf unit on the desk. You can also build independent storage units such as a rolling cabinet, a cabinet with drawers for blueprints, or a wall unit with pigeonholes *(pages 84-85)*.

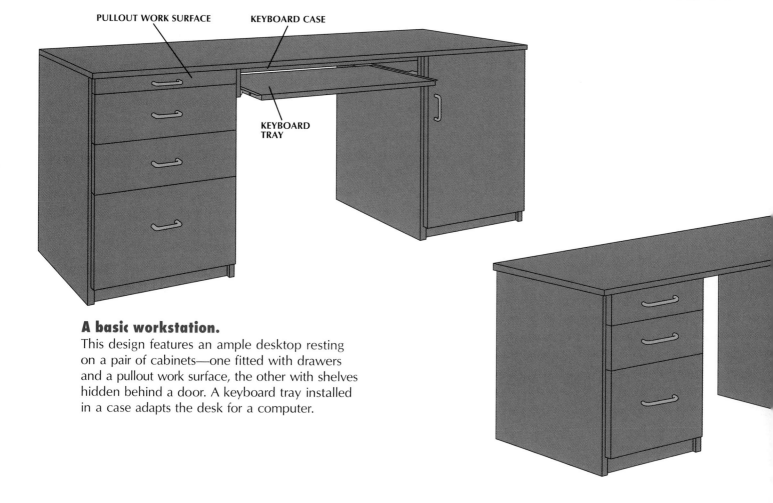

PULLOUT WORK SURFACE   **KEYBOARD CASE**

KEYBOARD TRAY

A basic workstation.

This design features an ample desktop resting on a pair of cabinets—one fitted with drawers and a pullout work surface, the other with shelves hidden behind a door. A keyboard tray installed in a case adapts the desk for a computer.

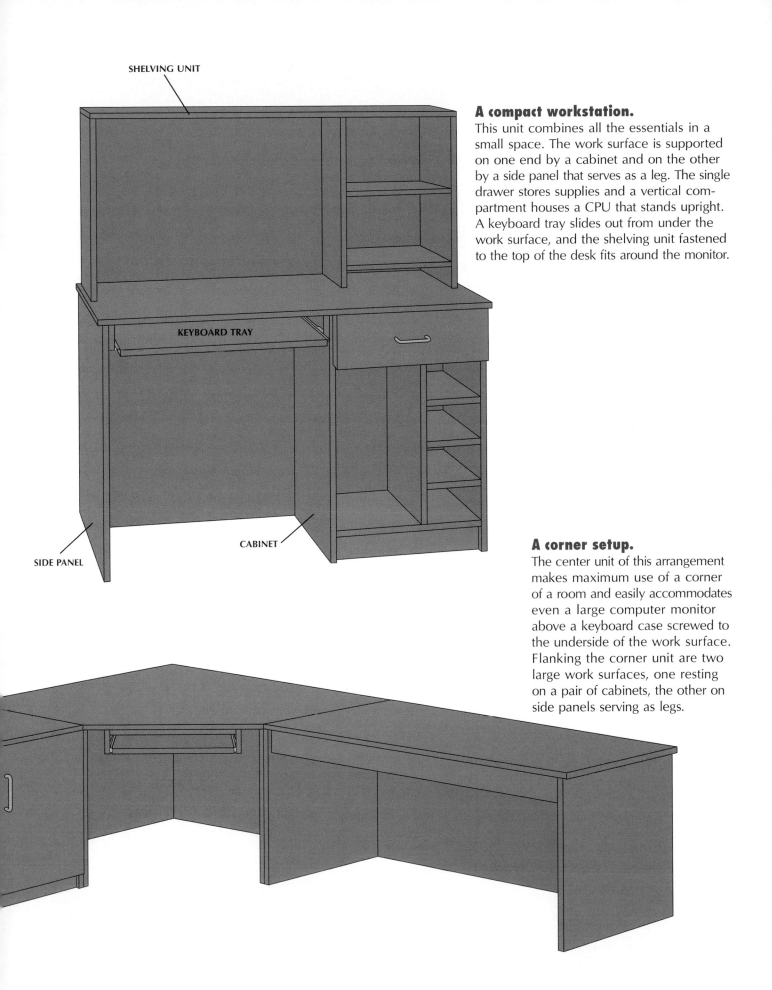

SHELVING UNIT

KEYBOARD TRAY

SIDE PANEL

CABINET

A compact workstation.

This unit combines all the essentials in a small space. The work surface is supported on one end by a cabinet and on the other by a side panel that serves as a leg. The single drawer stores supplies and a vertical compartment houses a CPU that stands upright. A keyboard tray slides out from under the work surface, and the shelving unit fastened to the top of the desk fits around the monitor.

A corner setup.

The center unit of this arrangement makes maximum use of a corner of a room and easily accommodates even a large computer monitor above a keyboard case screwed to the underside of the work surface. Flanking the corner unit are two large work surfaces, one resting on a pair of cabinets, the other on side panels serving as legs.

A rollout cabinet.

The desk shown at right is ideal for an office in a closet or other restricted space. Rather than resting on cabinets, the desk is freestanding, and a separate storage cabinet on casters is rolled underneath. The cabinet can be pulled out to serve as an extra work surface and tucked under the desk when not in use.

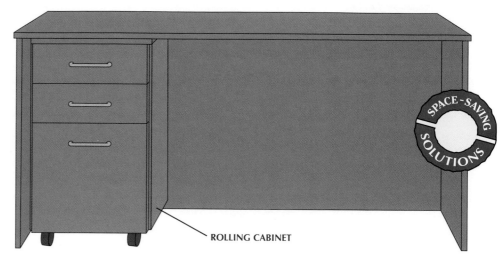

ROLLING CABINET

A mobile unit.

A wheeled workstation *(left)* can pack many features into a tiny space: a vertical compartment for a CPU; a desktop storage unit with space for a monitor; and a pullout keyboard tray that must extend far enough to provide knee and foot space. Mounting the printer shelf on drawer-glide hardware facilitates access to the top or back of the printer.

STORAGE UNIT

KEYBOARD TRAY

PRINTER SHELF

VERTICAL COMPARTMENT

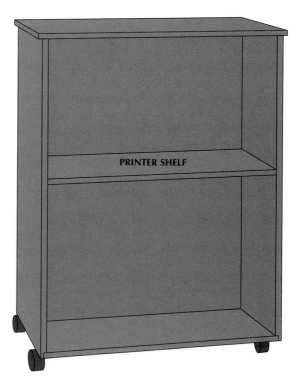

PRINTER SHELF

A rolling cabinet.

This unit is ideal for a printer and related supplies; the casters are handy for a printer that serves more than one computer. If your printer uses continuous-feed paper, thread the paper upward through a slot cut in the printer shelf.

Filing units.

These two wall-mounted units offer handy pigeon-holes for temporary filing. The unit with shallow shelves *(right)* is built much like a cabinet with adjustable shelves *(pages 94-99)*. For instructions on building the unit with vertical dividers *(below)*, turn to page 117.

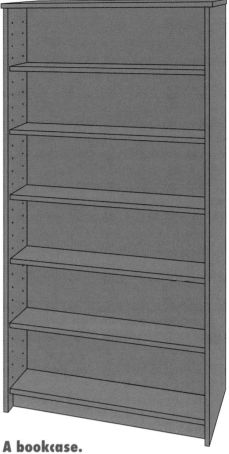

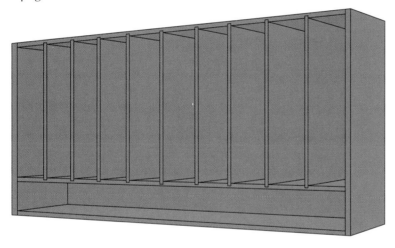

A bookcase.

This six-shelf unit is a variation of the cabinet with adjustable shelves shown on pages 94-97. The bookcase can be made any size as long as the shelf material can span the distance between the sides without bowing *(page 86)*.

EQUIPPING A SPACE FOR GRAPHIC ARTS OR SEWING

You can adapt the instructions in this chapter to build furniture specially suited to graphic design and sewing. For a graphic arts studio, it is best to buy a commercial drafting table, but you can build a cabinet *(right)* for storing photographs, artwork, or blueprints. Adapt the design on pages 94-97 and add shallow drawers *(pages 101-106)*.

To customize a desk *(page 82)* for a sewing machine, make the work surface at least 5 feet long and 18 to 24 inches deep. If you want the bed of the machine to sit flush with the table top, cut an opening in the surface and install brackets to hold a shelf sturdy enough to support the machine.

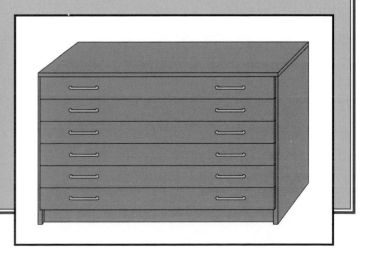

The highest quality furniture is made of solid wood. However, it is costlier than manufactured panels such as plywood or medium-density fiberboard (MDF). Moreover, solid wood is not generally available in widths over 12 inches, and many parts of a workstation are wider than this. To create a desktop of solid wood, for example, you would have to glue together several boards, edge to edge, to create a wide panel.

The Material of Choice: Available in 4- by 8-foot sheets, plywood and MDF are easier to work with than wood. Only MDF can be bought with a plasticlike coating, available in several colors, but both come in a variety of wood veneers. If you are planning to apply a stain or clear finish to your furniture, select an A-C grade for softwood veneer, A-2 for hardwood.

The material featured in this chapter is $\frac{3}{4}$-inch plywood. Although more expensive than MDF, it holds screws better and can span longer distances without sagging (chart, below). For the back panels of the cabinets that support the desktop, you may want to substitute $\frac{1}{8}$-inch hardboard.

Cutting the Pieces: The easiest way to cut large panels is with a circular saw (opposite). Smaller pieces can be cut on a table saw.

Before assembling your furniture, finish exposed edges with commercial edge banding—thin, self-adhesive strips of veneer applied with a household iron—or with solid wood (page 88).

 TOOLS

Chalk line	Clamps
Tape measure	Household iron
Circular saw	Hand roller
Plywood blade	Utility knife

 **MATERIALS**

Manufactured	Edge banding
panels	Sandpaper
2 x 4s	(medium-grade)

 SAFETY TIPS

Protect your eyes with goggles when using a circular saw.

MAXIMUM SPANS FOR MANUFACTURED PANELS

	½ inch	⅝ inch	¾ inch
Plywood	20 inches (24 inches for light loads)	28 inches (36 inches for light loads)	36 inches (48 inches for light loads)
MDF	16 inches (20 inches for light loads)	20 inches (36 inches for light loads)	24 inches (48 inches for light loads)

No-sag shelves and desktops.

The chart above suggests the maximum unsupported span for different thicknesses of plywood and MDF. Thin materials need supports spaced more closely than thick ones—as do heavy loads, which include items such as books and computer equipment. All the plywood and MDF in the chart can span greater distances if you strengthen it. To do so, double the material or fasten a 2-inch-wide strip of it to the underside of the shelf or desktop, stopping the strip short of desktop supports or shelf pegs.

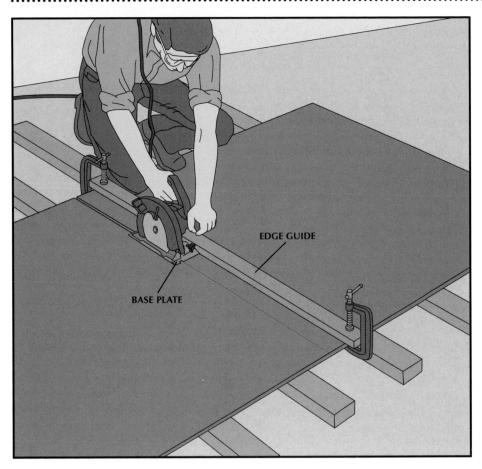

EDGE GUIDE

BASE PLATE

Using a circular saw.
To prevent plywood from splintering as you cut it, mount a plywood-cutting blade in your circular saw, apply a strip of masking tape across the panel before marking the cutting line with a chalk line, or score the cutting line with a utility knife.

◆ Support the panel on 2-by-4s spaced about a foot apart. Reposition the 2-by-4s as necessary to place one board 3 inches on each side of the cutting line.

◆ Measure the distance from the saw blade to the edge of the base plate and clamp a plywood or MDF strip as an edge guide this distance from the cutting line. Orient the guide with the factory-cut edge toward the cutting line. Hold the saw against the guide to confirm that the blade meets the cutting line.

◆ Kneeling on the panel over one of the 2-by-4s, cut the panel with the saw's base plate against the edge guide *(left)*.

TRICKS OF THE TRADE

A Circular-Saw Guide

A two-piece edge guide can be positioned at the cutting line, saving you the trouble of having to measure between the saw blade and base plate to position a guide. To make a guide for sawing a full-length manufactured panel, cut two 8-foot-long strips from the factory-cut edges of a $\frac{3}{4}$-inch plywood panel. (Four-foot strips make a guide that's more convenient for shorter cuts.) Make one strip 4 inches wide and the other 12 inches wide. Fasten the strips together with $1\frac{1}{4}$-inch No. 8 wood screws driven in a staggered pattern so the factory-cut edge of the narrow strip sits across the wider piece. Clamp the jig to a work surface, then cut the wide strip, holding the saw's base plate against the narrow strip *(below).* Varnish the jig to reduce warping. To use the jig, secure it with the sawed edge along the cutting line, extend the saw blade an inch, and run the saw base plate along the narrow strip.

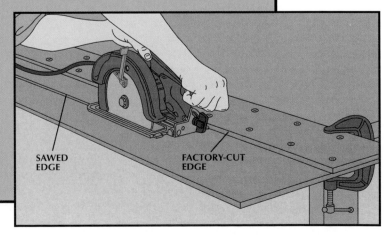

SAWED EDGE

FACTORY-CUT EDGE

EDGE TREATMENTS

Applying edge banding

◆ Support the panel vertically with clamps, and set a household iron to HIGH (without steam).

◆ Cut a strip of commercial banding slightly longer than the edge to be covered, and place the strip on the edge with the adhesive side down.

◆ Run the hot iron slowly along the edge, pressing the banding flat with one hand *(right)*; to prevent scorching the banding, avoid holding the iron in one spot for more than a few seconds.

◆ Applying even pressure, run a small block of wood or hand roller *(photograph)* back and forth along the edge.

◆ After the glue has set, turn the panel onto the banded edge, and run a utility knife along the adjacent face and edge to trim excess banding.

◆ Smooth the edges with medium-grade sandpaper.

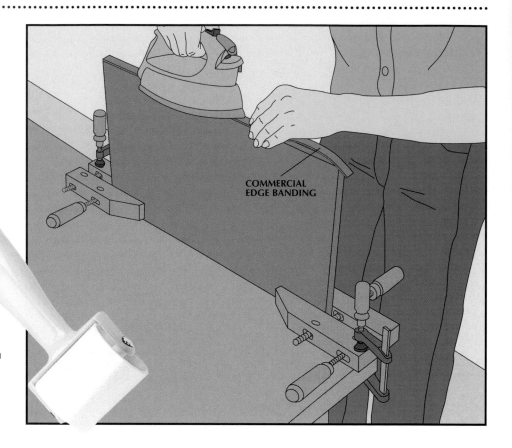

COMMERCIAL EDGE BANDING

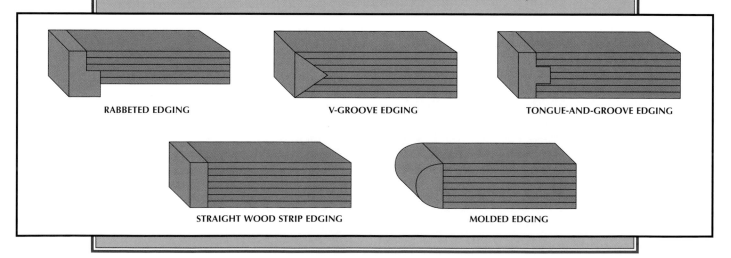

SOLID WOOD EDGING FOR PLYWOOD PANELS

Edging plywood or MDF panels with solid wood give you a broad choice of woods and decorative effects. As an added benefit, rabbeted edging also helps to reinforce the edge of the panel. Order custom-made edging from a lumber dealer, then for rabbeted, V-groove, or tongue-and-groove edging, cut the panel edge with a router to accept the shape. Fasten the edging with wood glue, clamping it firmly until the glue dries.

RABBETED EDGING

V-GROOVE EDGING

TONGUE-AND-GROOVE EDGING

STRAIGHT WOOD STRIP EDGING

MOLDED EDGING

There are several ways to fasten the panels of your workstation together. You can use screws *(below and pages 94-124)*, but dowel joints and plate joints also work well for plywood and medium-density fiberboard (MDF) panels. Metal brackets are suitable if they can be concealed *(page 93)*.

Joining with Screws: In furniture construction screws are usually countersunk—driven so the heads are flush with the surface. For a more finished look, you can conceal the fasteners completely by counter-boring the holes; this involves driving the screw heads below the surface and filling the holes with wood plugs, available in hardware stores precut in a variety of diameters. Select plugs in a contrasting wood, or stain them to match. A combination bit *(below)* drills the pilot, countersunk, and counter-bored holes, all in one operation.

Purchase flooring screws to connect the panels; they are less likely to split the material than standard wood screws. To join two boards face to face, use screws $\frac{1}{4}$ inch shorter than the combined thickness of the two pieces. For a right-angle joint, 2-inch screws offer a strong hold. The $\frac{5}{8}$-inch wood screws used to install hardware do not require pilot holes; make starting holes with an awl.

Biscuits for Strength: Plate joints are glued joints reinforced by oval wood wafers—called biscuits—inserted into semicircular slots cut into the mating pieces *(pages 92-93)*. You will need a plate joiner to make the slots, but the technique is simple to master, and the resulting joints are invisible and exceptionally strong.

The biscuit size depends on the thickness of the stock—$\frac{3}{4}$-inch wood requires No. 10 biscuits, for example. The plate joiner is adjustable to cut slots of the appropriate size.

Dowel Joints: Glued into holes drilled in the mating pieces *(pages 90-91)*, dowels also yield a joint that is invisible and easy to make, but not as strong as screws or biscuits. Pointed metal dowel centers make it easy to mate the panels exactly *(page 91)*. Use grooved dowels 1 to $1\frac{1}{2}$ inches long with a diameter no more than half the thickness of the stock.

 TOOLS

Bar clamps
Electric drill
Combination bit
Stop collar
Screwdriver
Wood chisel
Doweling jig
Dowel centers
C-clamps
Mallet
Plate joiner

 **MATERIALS**

Flooring screws
Wood glue
Wood plugs
Sandpaper
(medium-grade)
Dowels
Wood biscuits

 SAFETY TIPS

Protect your eyes with goggles when drilling.

FASTENING WITH SCREWS

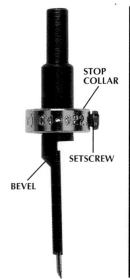

STOP COLLAR

SETSCREW

BEVEL

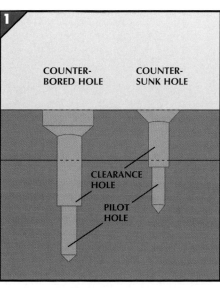

COUNTER-BORED HOLE

COUNTER-SUNK HOLE

CLEARANCE HOLE

PILOT HOLE

1. Hiding the screw heads.
Before drilling any screw holes, clamp the panels together as shown on pages 95 and 96.
◆ For a counterbored hole, position the stop collar on the shank $\frac{1}{4}$ inch above the beveled part of the shank *(photograph)*. For a countersunk hole, place the collar at the bevel. Tighten the setscrew to lock the collar in place, then install the bit in an electric drill and bore the holes.
◆ Disassemble the joint and spread a thin bead of wood glue on the mating surfaces.
◆ Reassemble the joint and drive a screw into each of the holes.

2. Hiding the screws.

◆ To conceal counterbored screws, buy wood plugs of the same diameter as the holes. Or, make your own plugs with a drill press equipped with a plug-cutting bit *(photograph)*.

◆ Squeeze a small amount of wood glue into the bottom of the hole. Push the plug into the hole and wipe up any excess glue with a damp cloth. Allow the glue to dry.

◆ With a wood chisel bevel side up, cut the plug flush with the surface *(right)*, then sand the surface smooth with medium-grade sandpaper.

PLUG CUTTER

MAKING DOWEL JOINTS

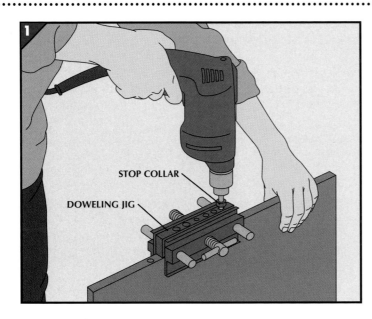

STOP COLLAR

DOWELING JIG

1. Drilling holes in one panel.

◆ Clamp one of the panels in a vise with the edge to be drilled facing up. Starting at one corner, mark the edge every 4 inches.

◆ Position a commercial doweling jig on the edge. Find the hole that matches the dowel diameter and center it on the first mark. Tighten the jig.

◆ Attach a stop collar or a piece of tape to the bit to mark the drilling depth equal to half the length of the dowel plus $\frac{1}{8}$ inch—plus the height of the doweling jig.

◆ Insert the bit through the jig and drill the hole.

◆ Bore the remaining holes *(left)*, repositioning the jig for each one.

TRICKS OF THE TRADE

A Handy Prop

You can hold a panel upright with simple wood props. Cut two short lengths of 2-by-6 stock, then make a slot halfway through each piece slightly wider than the thickness of the panels. To support a panel, fit a prop around each end of the piece.

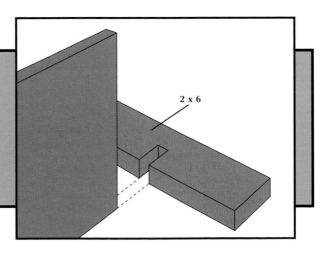

2 x 6

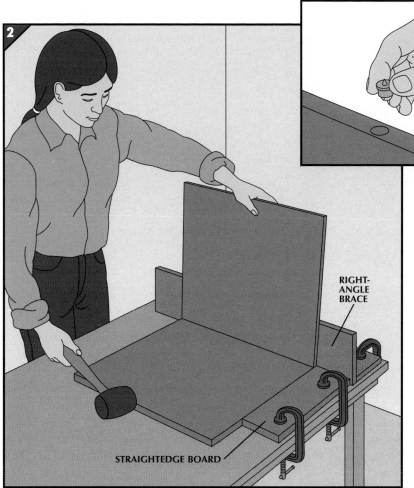

RIGHT-ANGLE BRACE

STRAIGHTEDGE BOARD

2. Marking the second panel.

Make a right-angle brace by fastening two boards together at a 90-degree angle. Clamp the brace to your worktable, then at a right angle to it, clamp a straightedge board to align the outside edges of the panels.

◆ Insert dowel centers into each of the holes drilled in the first piece *(inset)*.

◆ Hold the second panel upright against the brace, and set the drilled panel flat on the table.

◆ Tap the drilled panel with a rubber mallet, driving the dowel-center points into the vertical panel *(left)*.

◆ Drill holes in the second panel at the dowel-center marks as shown in Step 1.

◆ Repeat the process to drill holes for the remaining corners of the cabinet.

3. Joining the boards.

◆ Dab a little wood glue in the holes in one of the panels at each corner of the cabinet and insert the dowels loosely *(right)*.

◆ Drip glue in the holes of the other panels and spread a thin bead of glue on the mating surfaces.

◆ Orient the panels as in Step 2, lining up dowels with holes, and tap the corners together with a mallet.

◆ Clamp the cabinet as shown on page 95 until the glue has dried.

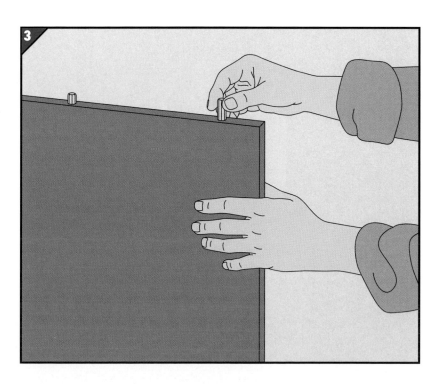

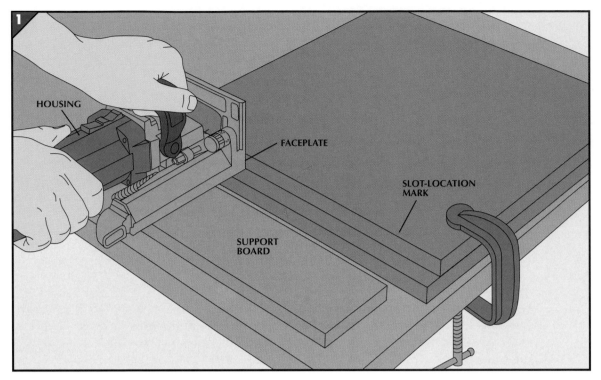

1. Cutting slots in the first panel.
◆ Lay one of the panels outside-face down on a work surface and set the other outside-face up on top of it. Mark reference letters to identify adjoining edges.
◆ Set the edge of the upper panel back by an amount equal to the thickness of the stock, then clamp the two pieces to the work surface.

◆ Place a support board the same thickness as the panels in front of the workpieces, then mark slot location lines on the top panel every 6 inches.
◆ Resting the plate joiner on the support board, align the guideline on its faceplate with a slot location mark on the stock. Holding the tool with both hands, push in the housing to cut the slot *(above)*. Repeat the process at the other marks.

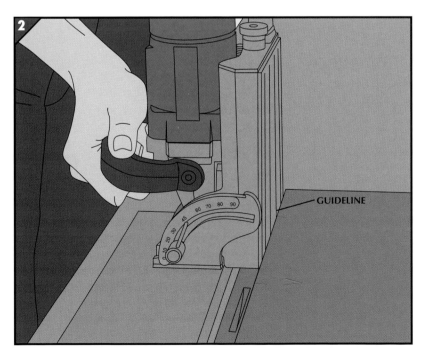

2. Slotting the second panel.
◆ Holding the plate joiner upright, align the guideline in the center of the tool's base plate with a slot mark and make a cut.
◆ Cut the rest of the grooves along the edge in the same way *(left)*.
◆ Mark slot-location points on the other three corners of the carcass, then cut slots at the marks.

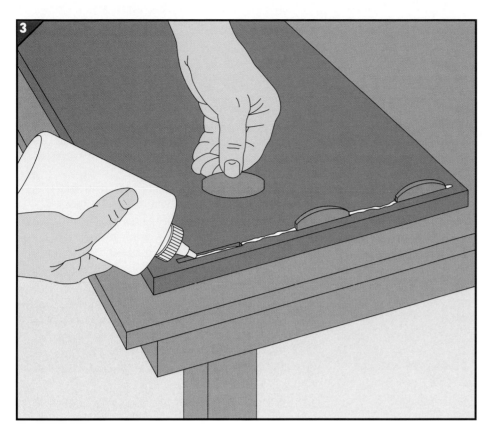

3. Inserting the biscuits.

◆ Set the panels with slots in their faces on a table, and squeeze a bead of wood glue into each slot and along the surface of the panels between the slots, inserting biscuits as you go *(left)*.

◆ Apply glue to the slotted edges of the other panels.

◆ Press the pieces together and clamp the cabinet as shown on page 95 until the glue has dried.

JOINING WITH METAL BRACKETS

Sturdy joints can be made with metal angle irons, although this method is best reserved for areas where the brackets will not be visible, such as an inside corner. For a very tight joint, attach the angle iron to one piece, setting it in slightly from the edge *(right)*. Then fasten the angle iron to the second piece—the panels will be pulled tightly together as you drive the screws.

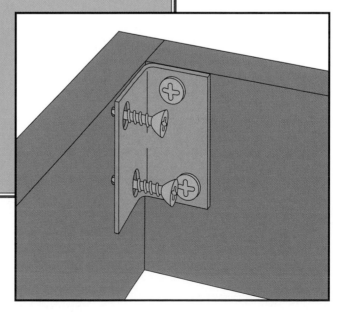

Assembling a Cabinet

Intended primarily to serve as a support for one end of a desktop, the cabinet shown below can also stand alone as a storage unit or bookcase. In that role it can provide a surface for equipment such as a fax machine or printer. This versatile unit can accommodate any combination of shelves, vertical dividers, drawers, or doors *(pages 98-108)*.

Planning: This cabinet can be made virtually any size. If it will help support a desktop, decide on the size of the top first, then make the cabinets 3 inches shallower so the top overhangs 2 inches at the back and 1 inch in front. Design the cabinets $\frac{3}{4}$ inch shorter than the desired height of the desk to allow for the top's thickness. In addition, plan for a top long enough to provide space for legroom and a keyboard tray between the cabinets.

If you plan to install shelves, consider the maximum span of the shelf material *(page 86)* in establishing the cabinet width. Where you intend to add a vertical divider for a CPU *(page 100)*, make the cabinet deep enough to allow 3 inches of space behind the unit for air circulation. If doors are part of the design, keep in mind that doors wider than 20 inches tend to sag on their hinges.

Building the Cabinet: Cut all the panels to size from $\frac{3}{4}$-inch plywood *(page 87)*, and install edging on each piece *(page 88)*. You can make the back from $\frac{1}{8}$-inch hardboard *(page 97)*. Then assemble the cabinets using one of the joinery methods described on pages 89 to 93.

 TOOLS

Tape measure
Circular saw
Electric drill

Combination bit
Screwdriver
Bar clamps
Combination square
Hammer

 **MATERIALS**

Plywood ($\frac{3}{4}$")
Hardboard ($\frac{1}{8}$")
Finishing nails (1")

Flooring screws
 (1", $1\frac{1}{4}$", 2" No. 8)
Wood screws ($\frac{5}{8}$" No. 6)
Angle irons (1" x 2")
Wood glue

 SAFETY TIPS

Protect your eyes with goggles when drilling and nailing.

Anatomy of a cabinet.
This simple cabinet is basically a box, or carcass, with two sides, a top, a bottom, and a back. Tack a hardboard back to the edges of the other panels. A plywood back can be recessed $\frac{1}{2}$ inch as shown here. The result is a more appealing cabinet, especially in settings where the back is exposed.

The bottom of the cabinet is anchored to cleats fastened inside the side panels. A kickplate set in $\frac{1}{2}$ inch from the front conceals the cleats and also supports the bottom. For a freestanding cabinet, add a false top that is about 1 inch larger than the cabinet on all sides.

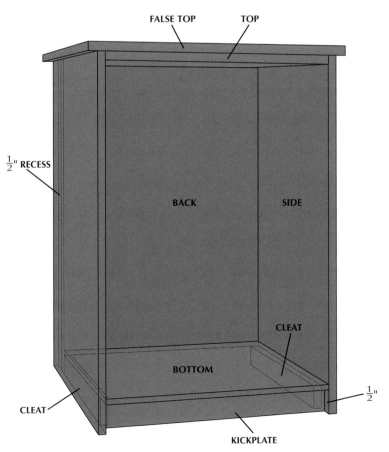

BUILDING THE CARCASS

1. Making the sides.

◆ From $\frac{3}{4}$-inch plywood, cut side panels the planned height and depth of the cabinet, then finish the edges *(page 88)*. Also cut two cleats 2 inches wide and $2\frac{1}{2}$ inches shorter than the width of the sides.

◆ Lay one side panel flat, inside face up. Position the cleat flush with the bottom of the panel and set in $1\frac{1}{4}$ inches from its front edge.

◆ Drill three pilot holes for $1\frac{1}{4}$-inch No. 8 flooring screws through the cleat, one near each end and one at the center.

◆ With glue and screws, fasten the cleat to the side panel *(right)*.

◆ Attach the other cleat to the opposite side panel in the same way.

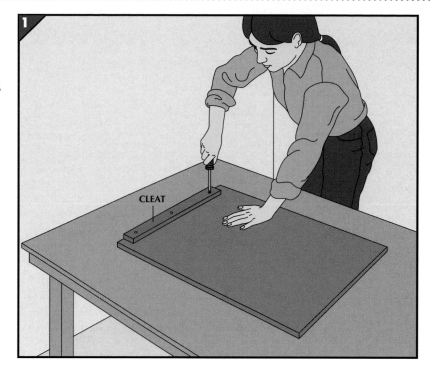

CLEAT

2. Squaring the carcass.

◆ Cut the top and bottom panels to size, making them $1\frac{1}{2}$ inches narrower than the width of the cabinet. For a hardboard back, make the top and bottom panels the same depth as the side panels. For an inset plywood back, cut them $1\frac{1}{4}$ inches shallower than the side panels. Finish the panel edges *(page 88)*.

◆ With a helper, set the two side pieces upright with their front edges down and slip the top and bottom pieces between them so the bottom is resting against the cleats and the top is flush with the edges of the side pieces.

◆ Secure the assembly with four bar clamps, then measure the carcass diagonally in both directions *(left)*. Identical diagonal measurements indicate that the carcass is square. If it is not, loosen the clamps slightly and slide one jaw of each clamp outward at opposite corners *(inset)*, then tighten the clamps and measure the diagonals again.

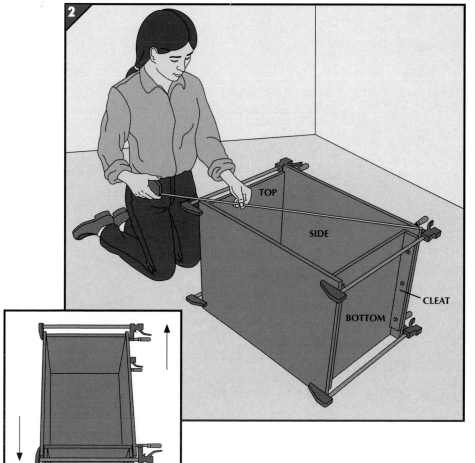

TOP

SIDE

CLEAT

BOTTOM

3. Marking pilot holes.

◆ Set a combination square to the distance between the bottom of the side panel and the center of the bottom panel edge.

◆ Holding the square against the bottom of the side panel, slide the head along the edge and lightly draw a line using the end of the ruler as a guide *(right)*.

◆ Mark the other side panel in the same way, then repeat the process to mark lines on the side panels in line with the top.

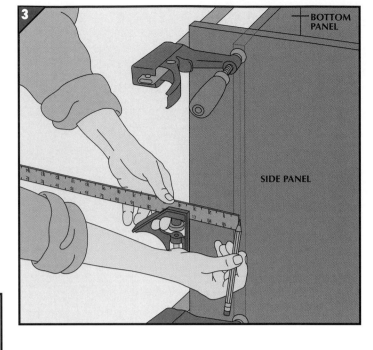

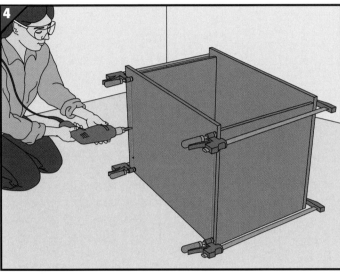

4. Drilling and fastening.

◆ At each marked line, drill pilot holes for counterbored flooring screws through the side panels and into the bottom panel, locating the holes about $1\frac{1}{2}$ inches from each end and every 6 inches in between.

◆ Drill pilot holes every 6 inches through the side panels into the top panel, then unclamp the carcass.

◆ With wood glue and screws, fasten the side panels to the top and bottom panels.

◆ Install clamps and re-check the carcass for square *(Step 2)*.

◆ Attach the back *(below or opposite)* before the glue dries completely.

INSTALLING THE BACK

A plywood back.

◆ Cut a $\frac{3}{4}$-inch plywood back to fit between the sides and to cover the rear edges of the top and bottom.

◆ Slide the back piece into place between the two side pieces *(right)*.

◆ Mark screw-hole lines on the back in line with the edges of the other panels, as in Step 3 above.

◆ Drill pilot holes for 2-inch No. 8 flooring screws through the back and into the top and bottom panels, and through the sides into

the back panel. Space the holes $1\frac{1}{2}$ inches from each end and every 6 inches in between.

◆ With glue and screws, fasten the back to the frame.

To add a false top, first drill a clearance hole for a 1-inch screw at each corner of the cabinet top. Then center the false top over the top, and from inside the cabinet, drill pilot holes up through the clearance holes into the false top. Screw the false top in place.

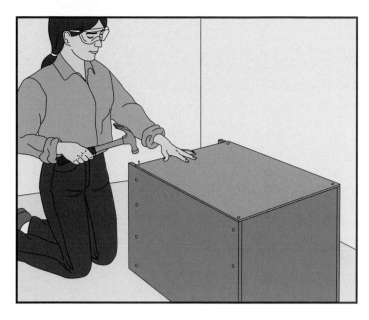

A hardboard back.

◆ Cut a piece of $\frac{1}{8}$-inch hardboard $\frac{1}{8}$ inch narrower than the cabinet and $\frac{1}{8}$ inch shorter than the distance from the top of the top panel to the bottom of the bottom panel.

◆ Set the back panel in place so it is slightly inset from the edges of the cabinet all around.

◆ Secure the back panel to one side panel with a 1-inch finishing nail driven into both corners, then add nails in the corners of the other side panel *(left)*.

◆ Drive nails every 3 inches around the perimeter of the back.

◆ Fasten the false top as described opposite *(bottom)*.

ADDING THE KICKPLATE

Attaching the angle irons.
◆ Turn the cabinet onto its back.
◆ Cut a kickplate from $\frac{3}{4}$-inch plywood 2 inches wide and long enough to fit between the side panels.
◆ Position the kickplate so it is resting on the ends of the cleats.
◆ With $\frac{5}{8}$-inch No. 6 wood screws, attach a 1- by 2-inch

angle iron to each cleat, setting it back slightly from the ends of the cleats *(page 93)*.
◆ Holding the kickplate down with one hand, screw the angle irons to the back of the kickplate *(right)*.
◆ Add a third angle iron, fastening the middle of the kickplate to the bottom panel.

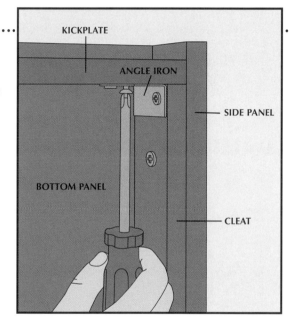

TRICKS OF THE TRADE

Keeping Everything Level

Uneven floors can make a perfectly square piece of furniture tilt or rock, but adjustable feet—consisting of a sleeve and a screw—will solve the problem. To install the feet at each corner, drill a hole in the bottom of the side panel slightly smaller than the sleeve and deep enough to accommodate the screw. To avoid splitting the wood, reinforce it with a C-clamp, protecting the surface with wood blocks. Tap the sleeve into place with a hammer *(right)*, then twist in the screw.

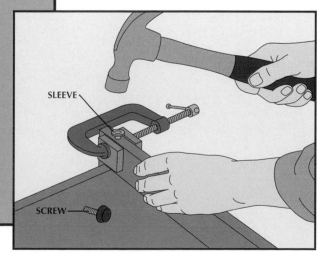

Storage space within your cabinet can be neatly organized with the addition of adjustable shelves. Putting in a vertical divider creates a separate compartment for a CPU. Building a larger cabinet and including shelves yields a bookcase.

Versatile Shelving: Installing adjustable shelves allows you to change the shelf spacing after the cabinet has been assembled. Simply drill two rows of holes into each side of the cabinet and insert shelf-support pegs or clips into the holes at the desired height. To ensure that each pair of holes is drilled at exactly the same height, use a hole-spacing jig *(below and opposite)*. Cut shelves to fit between the side panels.

A Vertical Divider: Create a separate compartment for a CPU by installing a vertical divider from the bottom of the cabinet to a fixed shelf near the top *(page 100)*. To prevent the CPU from overheating, the cabinet must be deep enough to allow for 3 inches of space behind the unit. Make the compartment 2 inches higher and wider than the CPU. For increased storage space, add shelves on one side of the compartment and build a drawer above it.

 TOOLS

Circular saw	Combination bit
Marking gauge	C-clamps
Electric drill	Corner clamp
Stop collar	Screwdriver

 **MATERIALS**

Plywood ($\frac{3}{4}$")	Wood glue
Shelf-support pegs	Flooring screws ($1\frac{1}{2}$" No. 8)

 SAFETY TIPS

Protect your eyes with goggles when you are drilling.

INSTALLING SHELVING

1. Making a hole-spacing jig.
◆ Cut a strip of $\frac{3}{4}$-inch plywood 4 inches wide and as long as the inside height of the cabinet. Mark an arrow at one end of the jig to indicate the top.
◆ Adjust a marking gauge to half the width of the strip and mark a line down the center *(right)*.
◆ Starting at the bottom, mark the centerline at 1-inch intervals and drill a hole through the jig at each mark, the same diameter as your shelf pegs.

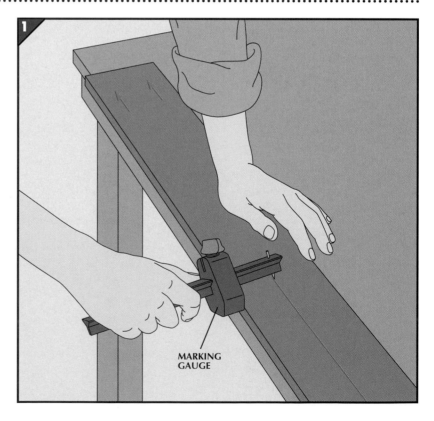

MARKING GAUGE

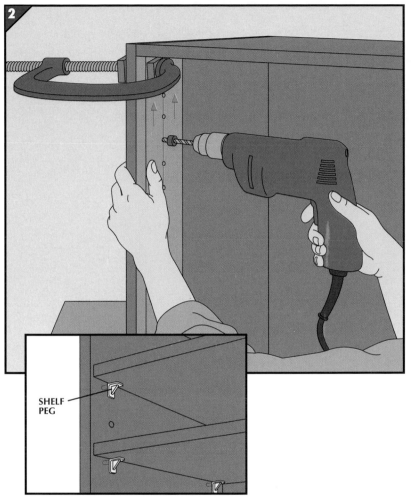

SHELF PEG

2. Drilling the holes in the cabinet sides.

◆ Add a stop collar or a piece of tape to the bit to mark the drilling depth—the thickness of the jig plus the length of the shelf-peg shafts.

◆ Clamp the jig to one side of the panel, with an edge flush against the front of the cabinet, and the correct end pointing up.

◆ Drill through each hole in the jig *(left)*.

◆ Repeat the procedure at the remaining three corners of the cabinet.

◆ From $\frac{3}{4}$-inch plywood, cut the shelves to fit between the cabinet sides; make them $\frac{1}{8}$ inch shallower than the depth of the cabinet so they will be set back from the front. Finish exposed edges *(page 88)*.

◆ Push shelf pegs into the holes at the desired height and install the shelves *(inset)*.

A COMMERCIAL HOLE-DRILLING JIG

The jig shown here will make quick work of drilling evenly spaced shelf-support holes. The wood strip is held against the front edge of a cabinet side panel, with the clear plastic template on the inside face. Starting at the bottom, holes are drilled through one of the two rows of holes in the jig. (To vary the location of the holes in relation to the cabinet edge, the wood strip can be attached to the opposite edge of the template.) When the last hole at the top has been drilled, the jig is moved up and a shelf-support peg is slipped through the appropriate-size index hole into one of the drilled holes to align the jig. The remaining holes are drilled, then the procedure is repeated at the back edge of the panel, and at both edges of the opposite side panel.

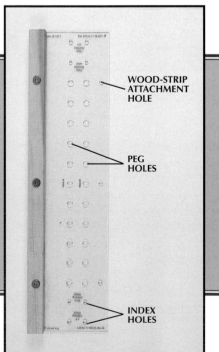

WOOD-STRIP
ATTACHMENT
HOLE

PEG
HOLES

INDEX
HOLES

A CPU compartment.

A cabinet supporting a desktop will likely provide more than enough space to accommodate a vertical CPU. The compartment can be cut off at the top by a fixed shelf, which will allow you to use the space above the CPU as a shelf or a drawer. The cavity beside the CPU can be fitted with small adjustable shelves; be sure to drill the shelf-support holes *(pages 98-99)* in the divider before installing it.

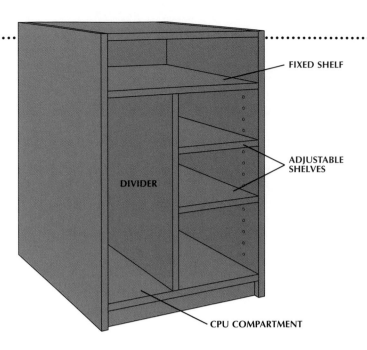

FIXED SHELF

ADJUSTABLE SHELVES

DIVIDER

CPU COMPARTMENT

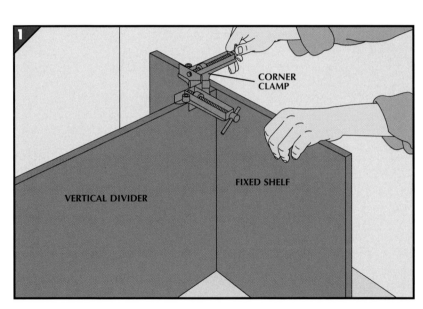

CORNER CLAMP

FIXED SHELF

VERTICAL DIVIDER

1. Joining the divider and shelf.

◆ From $\frac{3}{4}$-inch plywood, cut a shelf to fit between the sides of the cabinet, then cut the divider to fit between the bottom of the cabinet and the shelf. Finish exposed edges *(page 88)*.
◆ Set the two pieces on edge and fasten them together with a corner clamp *(left)*.
◆ Mark a line for screw holes across the shelf centered on the divider *(page 96, Step 3)*.
◆ Drill pilot holes for $1\frac{1}{2}$-inch No. 8 counterbored flooring screws through the shelf into the divider, locating the screws $1\frac{1}{2}$ inches from each edge and every 6 inches in between.
◆ With glue and screws, fasten the shelf to the divider.

2. Installing the assembly.

◆ Set the cabinet on its back and insert the shelf-and-divider assembly.
◆ Mark lines for screw holes across the sides and along the bottom, as described on page 96.
◆ Drill counterbored pilot holes through the sides of the cabinet into the fixed shelf *(right)* and through the bottom of the cabinet into the divider; locate the holes $1\frac{1}{2}$ inches from each edge and every 6 inches in between.
◆ Fasten the assembly to the cabinet with glue and screws.

Building Drawers

Fitting a small cabinet with drawers provides storage for files and supplies. A large cabinet with shallow drawers can be used to store photographs, artwork, or blueprints.

Drawer Design: A drawer is little more than a box consisting of four sides and a bottom. In addition, the simplest drawer to make has a false front that overlaps the frame of the cabinet *(below)*, concealing any imperfections in the fit. When planning the size of desk drawers, you'll need to make them slightly narrower than the opening in the cabinet to allow for drawer glides; this clearance will vary with the type of glide used.

Drawers can be made any height to accommodate the contents. File drawers and other tall drawers go at the bottom of the cabinet. To reduce weight, cut drawer sides only 6 inches high, then make a false front the height of a drawer insert *(box, page 103)*.

Making Drawers: Cut the front, back, and sides from $\frac{3}{4}$-inch plywood, and the bottom from $\frac{1}{8}$-inch hardboard. To withstand the stresses of being opened and closed, doors are typically built with stout joinery, which incorporates grooves called dadoes and rabbets. It's best to assemble the drawers *(pages 102-103)* before attaching the hardware and aligning the false fronts.

Drawer Hardware: Commercial drawer glides are the simplest way to install drawers in a cabinet. One part of the glide is attached to the drawer, and the other fastens to the side of the cabinet; interlocking channels on the glides enable the drawer to slide smoothly. To install file drawers, use special full-extension glides. These glides consist of three telescoping channels. They allow the drawer to be pulled out far enough for you to reach the back of the drawer.

TOOLS

Tape measure	Hammer
Circular saw	Screwdriver
Table saw or router	Hand-screw
Bar clamps	clamps
Electric drill	Combination
Combination bit	square

MATERIALS

Plywood ($\frac{3}{4}$")	Flooring screws
Hardboard ($\frac{1}{8}$")	($1\frac{1}{4}$", 2" No. 8)
Drawer glides	Spiral or coated
Drawer pulls	common
Wood glue	nails (1")

SAFETY TIPS

Wear goggles when you are nailing or when using an electric drill or power saw.

Anatomy of a drawer.

The front and back sit in rabbets cut in the sides. The hardboard bottom fits into dadoes cut $\frac{1}{4}$ inch from the bottom edges of the front and sides; the back is trimmed even with the top of the dadoes to allow the bottom to slide into place from the back of the drawer. The height of the false front depends on the contents planned for the drawer.

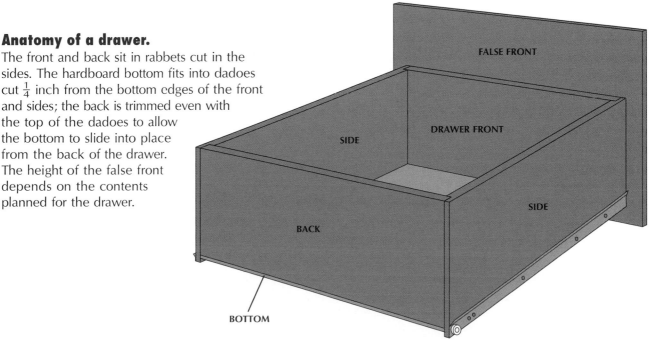

Positioning the drawer glides.

◆ First, determine the number of drawers (right) you want in the cabinet and the height of their false fronts. Size each false front so that it extends $\frac{1}{4}$ inch below the bottom of the drawer. In addition, leave a $\frac{1}{8}$-inch gap between the fronts and a $\frac{1}{8}$-inch reveal around the cabinet frame.

◆ To mark the position of the drawer glides on the cabinet frame, start with the bottom drawer: Measure the distance from the lower edge of the glide to the screw holes, add $\frac{1}{4}$ inch, and draw a line that distance above the cabinet bottom on both interior side panels.

◆ For the second drawer, measure the height of the bottom drawer's false front and subtract $\frac{1}{2}$ inch. Draw a line that distance above the first line.

◆ To mark the glide position of all other drawers, measure the height of the false front directly below and add $\frac{1}{8}$ inch.

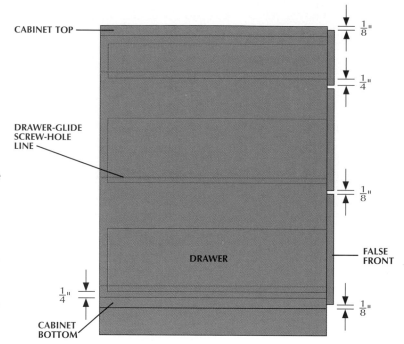

ASSEMBLING THE DRAWER

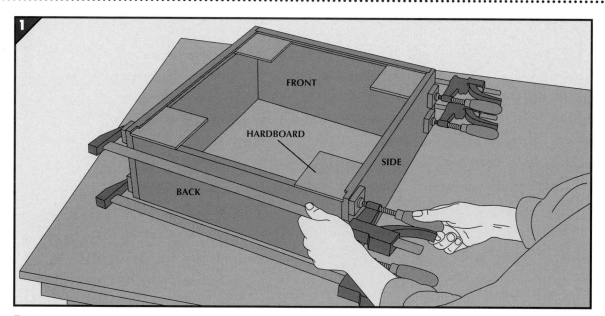

1. Clamping the pieces together.

◆ From $\frac{3}{4}$-inch plywood, cut the drawer sides the desired height and $\frac{1}{4}$ inch shorter than the depth of the cabinet.

◆ With a table saw or router, cut a rabbet at each end of the sides, $\frac{1}{8}$ inch deep and $\frac{3}{4}$ inch wide.

◆ Cut the drawer front to the same height as the side pieces, and the back piece $\frac{3}{8}$ inch narrower to allow the drawer bottom to slide in. Measure the cabinet opening, then subtract $1\frac{1}{4}$ inches (to account for the thickness of the two rabbeted side pieces) plus the clearance specified for the drawer glide. Trim both pieces to that width.

◆ Cut a dado $\frac{1}{4}$ inch deep and $\frac{1}{8}$ inch wide along the inside faces of the front and side pieces, $\frac{1}{4}$ inch from the bottom edges. Finish exposed edges (page 88).

◆ Assemble the drawer upside down on a worktable, slip small squares of $\frac{1}{8}$-inch hardboard into each corner, then clamp the drawer with four bar clamps (above).

◆ Drill pilot holes for 2-inch No. 8 counterbored flooring screws through the sides into the front and back pieces.

◆ With the hardboard squares in place, fasten the front, sides, and back with glue and screws.

2. Adding the bottom.

◆ Cut a piece of $\frac{1}{8}$-inch hardboard to fit in the grooves in the drawer sides and front, then slide it into place *(left)*.

◆ With 1-inch spiral or coated common nails, fasten the bottom to the edge of the drawer back, spacing the nails every 3 inches.

A SUPPORT FOR HANGING FILES

An ordinary drawer of the appropriate size can be equipped for hanging files with a commercial insert like the one shown here. Some models are adjustable to accommodate either letter- or legal-size files. For legal-size files, change the orientation of the insert, or of the files, so they run from back to front instead of side to side.

INSTALLING DRAWER GLIDES

1. Attaching the cabinet hardware.

◆ Determine the location of the drawer glides *(page 102)* and mark a line for each glide across the cabinet side.

◆ Separate a drawer glide into its pieces and set the one that attaches to the cabinet against the side panel so the screw holes are centered on the marked line. Fasten it with the screws provided *(right)*.

◆ Screw the remaining glides to the cabinet side in the same way.

For a file drawer, engage the mating glides with those in the cabinet and pull them all the way out until they lock *(inset)*.

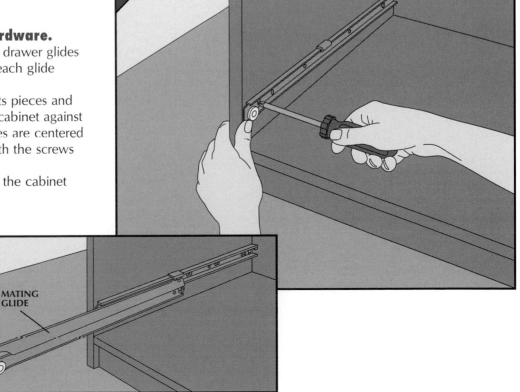

MATING GLIDE

2. Fitting glides on the drawers.

◆ Position the drawer glide on the drawer according to the manufacturer's instructions; for the model shown, the channel is positioned flush with the front of the drawer and the wheel at the back.

◆ Fasten the glide to the drawer through the oblong screw holes with the screws provided *(right)*.

◆ Test-fit the drawer in the cabinet; it should slide smoothly. If not, loosen the screws and move the channel sideways slightly.

◆ When the glides are well adjusted, drive screws through the remaining holes.

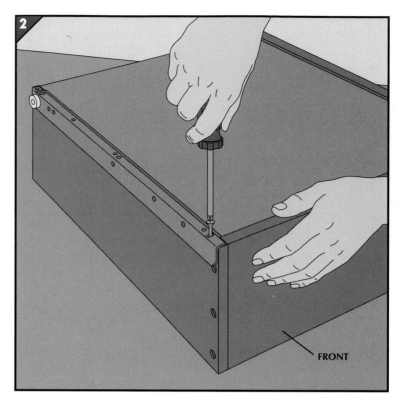

FRONT

ADDING THE FALSE FRONTS

WOOD BLOCK

1. Positioning the first piece.

◆ Cut the drawer false fronts to the desired size *(page 102)* and finish exposed edges *(page 88)*.

◆ Install the bottom drawer and pull it partway out. Set two blocks of wood cut $\frac{1}{8}$ inch higher than the top of the kick-plate installed earlier at the bottom of the cabinet.

◆ Set the false front on the blocks and, resting it against the front of the drawer, draw a line along the top of the drawer on the back of the false front *(left)*.

2. Fastening the false front.

◆ Remove the drawer and place it on the false front, centering it between the edges and aligning the top of the drawer with the marked line.
◆ Secure the pieces with hand-screw clamps.
◆ Drill pilot holes for $1\frac{1}{4}$-inch No. 8 countersunk flooring screws through the drawer front into the false front. Locate one row of holes 1 inch from the top of the drawer and another row 1 inch from the bottom, spacing the holes 1 inch from each end and every 6 inches in between.
◆ Drive the screws *(right)*.

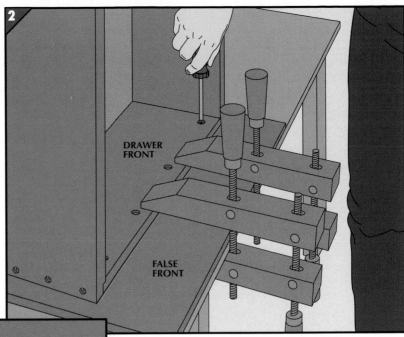

3. Positioning the remaining pieces.

◆ Install the bottom drawer in the cabinet, then slide in the second drawer.
◆ Pull the two drawers out partway, and stack two quarters on the false front of the bottom drawer near each end, creating a $\frac{1}{8}$-inch gap between the false fronts.
◆ Set the second false front on the quarters, aligning it with the one below *(left)*, and draw a line along the top of the drawer on the back face of the false front.
◆ Fasten the second false front to the drawer *(Step 2)*.
◆ Attach the remaining false fronts in the same way.

TRICKS OF THE TRADE

Aligning the Front with Brads

To facilitate the positioning of a false front, set the drawer face up and drive two brads into the drawer front, leaving the heads protruding. (Make sure not to place the brads where the drawer handle will be installed.) Snip off the ends of the brads with pliers *(right)*. Install the drawer and position the false front *(Step 1, opposite)*, pressing it against the brads on the front of the drawer. Remove the drawer and fasten the false front *(Step 2, above)*, using the indentations left by the brads to place the false front correctly.

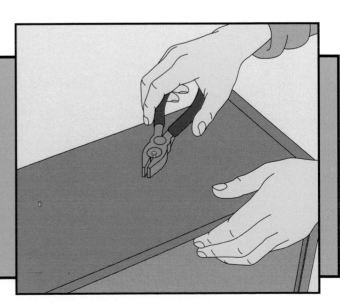

ATTACHING DRAWER PULLS

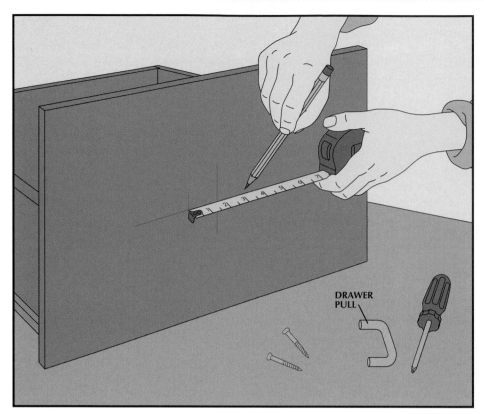

DRAWER PULL

Placing the hardware.
◆ With a tape measure and combination square, locate and mark the center of the false drawer front with two crossing lines. If your drawer pull has a single fastener, drill a hole for it where the lines cross.

◆ For a two-fastener pull, measure the distance between the two screw holes on the drawer pull, divide the measurement by two, and mark this distance on each side of the center *(left)*.
◆ Drill a clearance hole into the false front and through the drawer front at each mark for the screws provided with the drawer pull.
◆ Holding the drawer pull in position against the false front, drive the screws from the inside to fasten the pull to the drawer.

A HIDDEN WORK SURFACE

Expand a desk's work space by including a pullout "breadboard" in the top of a cabinet supporting a desktop. The unit consists of a $\frac{3}{4}$-inch plywood rectangle cut as wide and as deep as a drawer and screwed to the top of a front tall enough for fastening a pull. A false front, cut to match the spacing of the drawer false fronts below it, conceals the seam and the top edge of the cabinet with a $\frac{1}{8}$-inch reveal. Mount the work surface in the cabinet so it clears the top by $\frac{1}{4}$ inch.

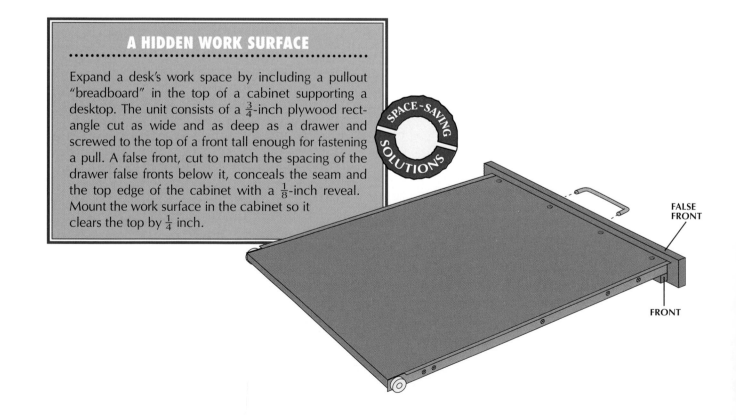

SPACE-SAVING SOLUTIONS

FALSE FRONT

FRONT

Doors can conceal the contents of a cabinet, hiding the clutter of office supplies. The simplest door to install is one that overlaps the front of the cabinet *(below)*, masking any minor errors in measurement and construction. The door can be made from the same $\frac{3}{4}$-inch plywood as the cabinet.

Types of Door Hinges: Spring-loaded hinges lock in the open position, and hold the door in place when it is closed, making a catch or latch unnecessary. A special kind of spring-loaded hinge—called a European hinge *(page 108)*—allows for easy adjustment if the door shifts or sags with time. For a cabinet that will support a desktop, install the door so it opens away from you when you are seated at the desk.

Hardware Requirements: The number and size of hinges required for a door depend on its dimensions. Two rules of thumb apply: First, for a door that is taller than 2 feet, install three hinges; second, make sure the total length of the hinges equals at least one-sixth the length of the door edge. For example, if the door is 24 inches high, use two 2-inch hinges.

When only two hinges are required, place them a quarter of the way from the top and bottom of the door; with three hinges, place one in the center and the other two 4 or 5 inches from the top and bottom.

TOOLS

Circular saw
Combination
 square
Screwdriver

MATERIALS

Plywood ($\frac{3}{4}$")
Hinges
Handle

SAFETY TIPS

When drilling, protect your eyes with goggles.

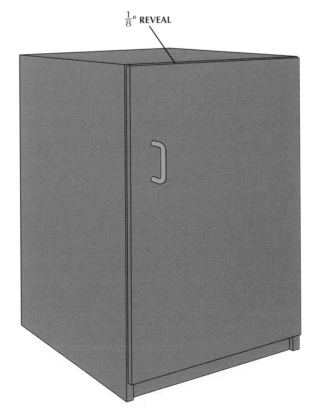

$\frac{1}{8}$" REVEAL

An overlapping door.
An overlapping door *(right)* is cut to fit over the cabinet front, inset $\frac{1}{8}$ inch from the sides, the top, and the top of the kickplate. Designed to hide small irregularities in the construction of the cabinet, this type of door is easier to fit than other styles. Its handle is attached in the same manner as a drawer pull *(page 106)*, but is positioned vertically near the unhinged edge of the door.

INSTALLING THE DOOR

1. Fastening hinges to the door.
◆ Cut a door from $\frac{3}{4}$-inch plywood, making it $\frac{1}{8}$ inch smaller all around than the front of the cabinet frame. Finish exposed edges *(page 88)*.
◆ With a combination square, mark a line along the inside face of the door, $\frac{5}{8}$ inch from the hinged edge.
◆ Position the hinges on the door along the line *(left)*.
◆ Fasten the hinges by driving the screws provided through the oblong holes.

2. Positioning the door.
◆ Set the door on wood blocks $\frac{1}{8}$ inch higher than the kickplate, and hold it partially open against the cabinet *(right)*.
◆ Have a helper open the hinges against the inside of the cabinet and mark the center of the oblong holes.
◆ Open the door completely, align the oblong holes with the marks, and drive the screws.
◆ Close the door and check its alignment. If necessary, adjust the door's position by loosening the screws attaching the hinges to the door or cabinet and adjusting the position of the hinges.
◆ When you are satisfied with the alignment, drive screws in the round holes.

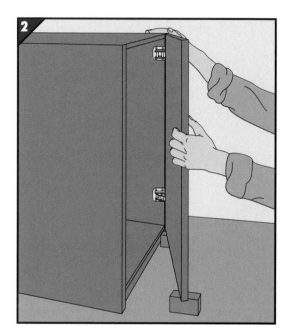

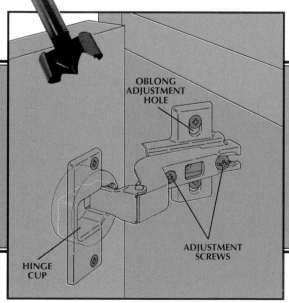

FORSTNER BIT

OBLONG ADJUSTMENT HOLE

ADJUSTMENT SCREWS

HINGE CUP

EURO-STYLE HINGES

Spring-loaded European hinges are easy to adjust in all directions. The cup on one leaf fits into a cavity drilled in the door with a Forstner bit *(photograph)*; the other leaf is screwed to the side of the cabinet. Oblong holes in the cabinet leaf allow the hinge to move up and down on its mounting screws. In-and-out adjustments are accomplished by turning the two screws in the hinge's center mechanism. You can remove the door by removing the adjustment screws and sliding the hinge leaves apart.

A cabinet on wheels can be easily stored under a desk or tucked into a corner of the room and rolled out when needed. The cabinet can be fitted with drawers—a mobile filing cabinet comes in very handy—or shelves, and is ideal for housing a printer.

The cabinet illustrated below is constructed in the same way as the one shown on pages 94 to 97, with a few exceptions. To provide a flat surface for fastening the casters, the sides are rabbeted to rest on the bottom and there is no kickplate.

Plate-style casters *(photograph)* are fastened to the bottom of the cabinet with screws. To simplify screwing the mounting plate to the cabinet, separate the plate from the wheels; if the two parts do not come apart, rotate the caster as necessary to reach the mounting screws. (Stem casters, comprising a shaft that slides into a sleeve inserted in a drilled hole, cannot be used with this piece.)

Choose casters with large wheels like those shown below rather than ones with a small rolling ball—the type with a wheel supports more weight. If you plan to store the cabinet under a desk, be sure to take into account the height of the wheels when determining the height of the cabinet.

A false top can be fastened to the top of the cabinet to serve as a work surface; be sure to include its thickness in determining the overall height of the cabinet.

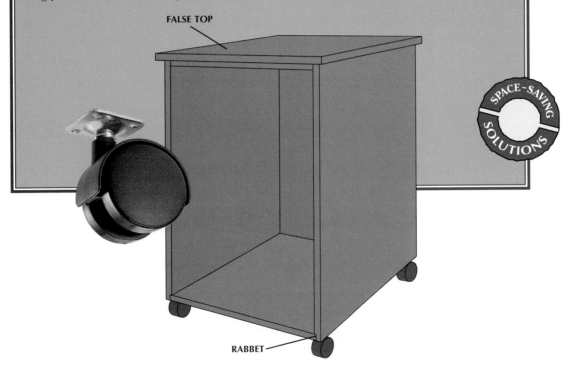

FALSE TOP

RABBET

Transforming a pair of small cabinets into a computer workstation calls for the addition of a desktop spanning the cabinets and a keyboard tray between them.

A standard desk work surface measures 30 by 60 inches. Make the top long enough to allow no less than 26 inches between cabinets.

Desktop Details: Depending on the material you are using and its thickness *(page 86)*, this distance may be too great for the top to span without reinforcement. You can stiffen the desktop with the rabbeted edging shown on page 88 or with a case for a keyboard tray screwed to the underside of the desktop *(page 112)*.

For an attractive look, design the top to overhang the front and sides of the cabinet. An overhang at the back leaves space behind the desk for plugging equipment into electrical receptacles.

Paths for Wires: In addition to a rear overhang, the desktop will also need openings for telephone and electrical wires, as will the back and sides of the cabinet.

The simplest solution is to cut holes through the panels and install a plastic grommet in each opening *(opposite)*. These grommets are available in a variety of sizes. You can also buy plastic clips and channels designed to guide wires along a desk or wall.

The Keyboard Tray: The tray is installed with drawer glides that lock in position when pulled all the way out. If the cabinets supporting the top are close enough together that reinforcement is not required, you can simply fasten the tray hardware to the sides of the cabinets. You can also purchase a commercial keyboard tray instead of building one yourself.

 TOOLS

Electric drill	Screwdriver
Combination bit	Circular saw
Hole-saw	Bar clamps
attachment	Hand-screw
C-clamps	clamps

 MATERIALS

Plywood ($\frac{3}{4}$")	Wood glue
Flooring screws	Plastic grommet
($1\frac{1}{4}$", 2" No. 8)	Drawer glides

 **SAFETY TIPS**

Protect your eyes with goggles when you are using power tools.

MOUNTING THE WORK SURFACE

Fastening the desktop to the cabinets.
◆ Position the two cabinets parallel to each other and the correct distance apart. Remove any drawers from them.
◆ Drill a clearance hole for a No. 8 flooring screw at each corner of the cabinet tops.
◆ Cut the top from $\frac{3}{4}$-inch plywood large enough to overlap the cabinets 1 inch on each side and 2 inches in back; in front, make the overlap 1 inch, or $\frac{1}{4}$ inch past the front of any drawers or doors. Finish exposed edges *(page 88)*.
◆ With a helper, position the desktop on the cabinets *(left)* and clamp it to them.
◆ From inside the cabinets, drill pilot holes for $1\frac{1}{4}$-inch No. 8 flooring screws up through the clearance holes into the underside of the top.
◆ Drive a screw up into each pilot hole.

CREATING PASSAGES FOR WIRES

Drilling openings.
◆ Mark the location of holes for wires and buy plastic grommets of the appropriate size *(photograph)*.
◆ Fit an electric drill with a hole-saw bit the same size as the grommet, then cut a hole at each marked location *(right)*.
◆ Press the plastic grommet into place.

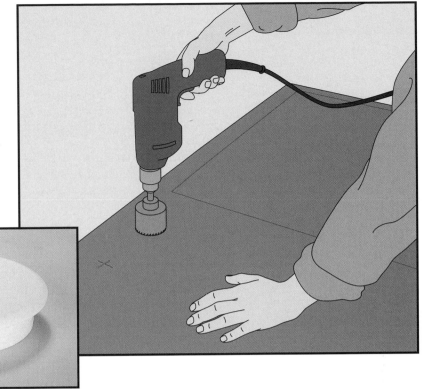

A TRACK FOR CONTROLLING CABLES

The many cables, wires, and power cords from home-office equipment can create an untidy tangle on the floor or behind a desk. This can also pose a tripping hazard. One of many commercial products for neatly routing this wiring along a desk or wall is the plastic track illustrated at right. Cut to length with a utility knife, the track is fastened to a sur-face with an adhesive strip attached to the back.

Avoid putting printer cables longer than 6 feet in the same track as a power cable, to prevent electrical interference.

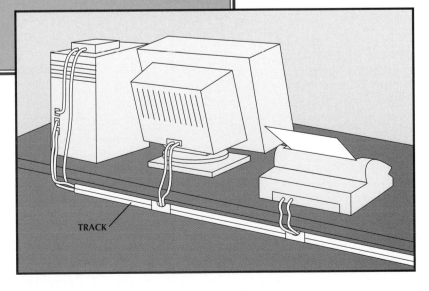

TRACK

INSTALLING A KEYBOARD TRAY

A keyboard tray in a case.

The keyboard tray at right fits in a case—a box without a front or bottom mounted to the underside of the desktop and to the cabinets. Built wide enough to span the distance between the cabinets, the case is also deep enough to accept locking drawer glides.

KEYBOARD TRAY

DRAWER GLIDE

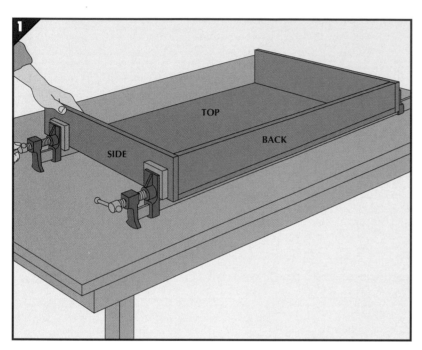

1. Assembling the case.

◆ Cut the two side pieces from $\frac{3}{4}$-inch plywood long enough to accommodate the depth of the keyboard tray, plus 3 inches for wires, and wide enough to hold the tray the desired distance below the top.

◆ Cut the top piece to a length equal to the distance between the cabinets less $1\frac{1}{2}$ inches, and to a width matching the length of the side pieces.

◆ Cut the back piece the same length as the top and $\frac{3}{4}$ inch narrower than the side pieces. Finish exposed edges of all the pieces *(page 88)*.

◆ Assemble the pieces with bar clamps *(left)*, protecting the stock with wood pads.

◆ Drill pilot holes for 2-inch No. 8 countersunk flooring screws through the sides into the top and back, spacing them every 6 inches.

◆ Fasten the pieces together with glue and screws, then turn the assembly over and countersink screws to fasten the top to the back.

2. Mounting the case and tray.

◆ Drill clearance holes for $1\frac{1}{4}$-inch No. 8 flooring screws 1 inch from the edges and every 6 inches around the perimeter of the top of the keyboard case, and every 6 inches through the sides of the keyboard case into the sides of the cabinet.

◆ Position the case under the top and secure it there with hand-screw clamps.

◆ Drill pilot holes into the underside of the top and the cabinet sides through the clearance holes.

◆ Drive screws through all the pilot holes *(right)*.

◆ Cut the keyboard tray from $\frac{3}{4}$-inch plywood, making it the depth of the case less 3 inches to accommodate wires, and the width of the case less the clearance required for drawer hardware. Finish the exposed edges *(page 88)*.

◆ Install locking drawer glides on the case and keyboard tray *(pages 103-104)*.

◆ Slide the keyboard tray into the drawer glides mounted in the case.

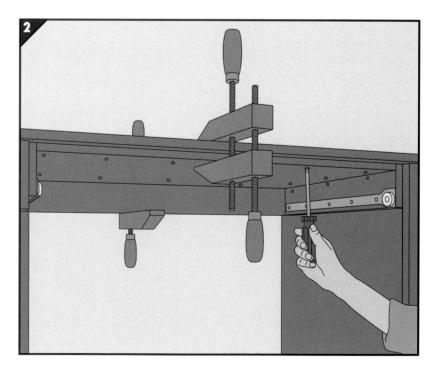

Fastening a top to a pair of cabinets is only one way to create a desk. You can also build a freestanding desk, supported by plywood legs, and design it to be rectangular or custom-made to fit into a corner. If you are planning to build more than one unit and place them side by side, ensure that the tops are all the same height and depth.

A Corner Unit: A five-sided desk unit *(below)* fits neatly into a corner, making efficient use of space in a small room. It can also be sized to fit between a pair of rectangular desks or cabinets no more than 30 inches deep and is an ideal spot for a computer monitor, freeing desk space on the other work sur-

faces. The open front edge of the desk can be fitted with a keyboard tray *(opposite)*.

A Rectangular Desk: A simple four-sided desk *(page 115)* can be designed in the same way as a small cabinet; the only difference is that the desk is built without a bottom. The desk can be made any size; if built just wide enough to accommodate a keyboard tray, it can serve as a compact computer workstation.

Finishing Touches: Useful additions to these desks include adjustable feet for leveling *(page 97)* and holes with grommets for routing wires *(page 111)*.

 TOOLS

Carpenter's
  square
Tape measure
Circular saw

Protractor
Straightedge
C-clamps
Electric drill
Combination bit
Screwdriver

 **MATERIALS**

Plywood ($\frac{3}{4}$")
Flooring screws
  (2" No. 8)
Angle irons
Wood glue

SAFETY TIPS

Put on goggles when using any power tool.

Anatomy of a corner unit.

The top of this desk is designed with two 48-inch edges that fit in a corner of a room, two short edges intended to butt against adjoining desk units, and a diagonal edge long enough to accommodate a keyboard tray. The back panels and the side panels are fastened to the edges of the top panel. For a freestanding unit, cut the false top to overhang the top panel as for the cabinet *(page 94)*. If it will abut a cabinet or desk, make the overhang dimensions the same on all the units but cut the false top flush with the side panels where the units meet. By doubling the thickness of the top, the false top reinforces the desk.

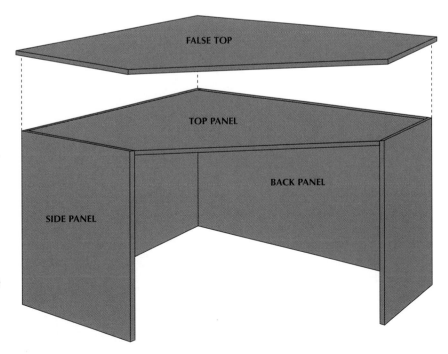

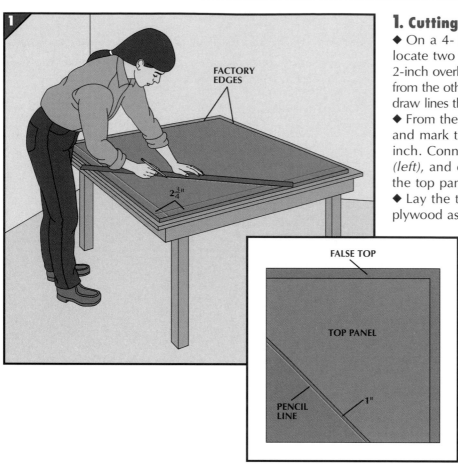

FACTORY EDGES

$2\frac{3}{4}''$

FALSE TOP

TOP PANEL

PENCIL LINE

1''

1. Cutting the desktop.

◆ On a 4- by 4-foot square of $\frac{3}{4}$-inch plywood, locate two factory edges that form a corner. For a 2-inch overhang near the wall, measure in $2\frac{3}{4}$ inches from the other two edges with a carpenter's square, and draw lines the length and width of the plywood square.

◆ From the factory edges, measure along each line and mark the depth of the adjoining units less $\frac{3}{4}$ inch. Connect these marks with a diagonal line *(left)*, and cut along all three lines to complete the top panel.

◆ Lay the top panel on another 4-foot square of plywood as shown in the inset. Measure out 1 inch— the amount of false-top overhang on the adjacent units—from the diagonal edge of the top panel and mark a parallel line on the lower plywood square.

◆ Cut along the line to complete the false top.

◆ Finish exposed edges *(page 88)*.

2. Attaching the side panels.

◆ Cut two side panels to the desired height, making their width equal to the length of the side edges of the top plus $\frac{3}{4}$ inch. Finish exposed edges *(page 88)*.

◆ Clamp the top to a work surface and have a helper hold one side panel in position against it, aligning the front edges of the two panels.

◆ Mark screw-hole lines on the side panel centered on the top panel, as shown on page 96.

◆ Drill counterbored pilot holes for 2-inch No. 8 flooring screws through the side panel into the top, locating the holes $1\frac{1}{2}$ inches from each edge and every 6 inches in between along the marked line *(right)*.

◆ Fasten the side panel to the top panel with glue and screws.

◆ Attach the opposite side panel in the same way.

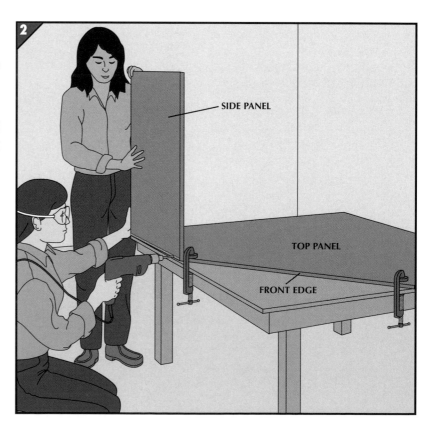

SIDE PANEL

TOP PANEL

FRONT EDGE

3. Adding the back panels.

◆ From ¾-inch plywood, cut a back panel the same height as the side panels and the width of one of the back edges of the top panel. Cut the second back panel ¾ inch wider.

◆ Working with a helper, position the wider panel against a back edge of the top panel so its edge is covered by a side panel (right).

◆ Drill pilot holes and fasten the panel as you did for the side panels (Step 2), driving the screws through the back panel into the top panel, and through the side panel into the back panel.

◆ Position the second back panel against the top panel between the first back panel and the side panel. Secure it to all three in the same way as the first back panel.

◆ Turn the base upright and fasten the false top to it in the manner shown on page 110.

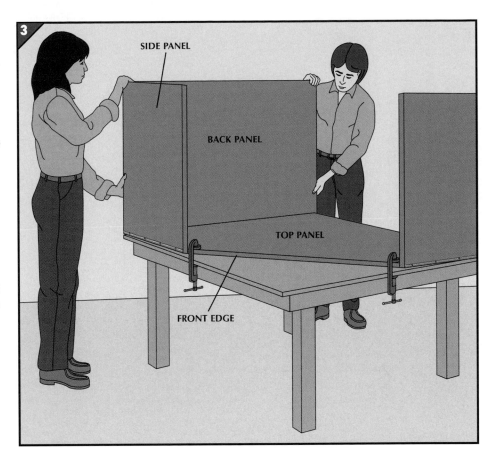

SIDE PANEL

BACK PANEL

TOP PANEL

FRONT EDGE

A RECTANGULAR DESK

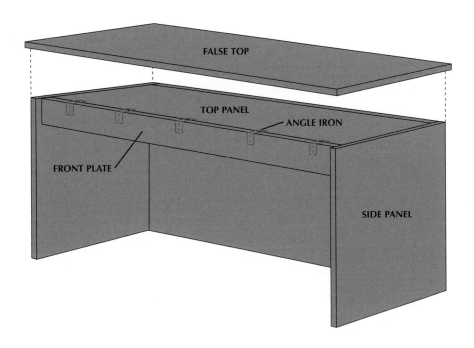

FALSE TOP

TOP PANEL

ANGLE IRON

FRONT PLATE

SIDE PANEL

Building the piece.

A rectangular desk can be assembled in the same way as a corner unit. Set the top panel on a work surface and, working with a helper to position the side panels, fasten them to the top. Cut the back panel to fit between the two side panels so that its edges are hidden. Fasten it to the top and the two side panels (page 114, Step 2). A front plate reinforces the top and gives the desk a more finished appearance. Fasten the plate to the desktop with angle irons spaced every foot. A false top—with overhanging edges as described on page 110—is then fastened to the base.

Shelving on or above a desk keeps office materials organized and frees precious desk space. A custom shelving unit can either be fastened to the desktop or mounted on the wall above it.

A Desktop Unit: You can design desktop shelves with compartments for a computer monitor and other equipment such as a printer. Consider including small doors and drawers to keep supplies out of sight. Such units usually span the full length of the desk; make it deep enough to accommodate its planned contents, but not so deep as to take up too much desk space. See that no shelf exceeds the maximum span for the material you are using *(page 86)*.

A Wall Unit: Wall-mounted shelving can be firmly fastened to the studs, or even tucked in between them *(opposite)*. Vertical cubbyholes keep temporary files sorted and readily accessible. It's a good idea to size shelf compartments for letter- or legal-size files.

 TOOLS

Table saw
Circular saw
Bar clamps

Electric drill
Combination bit
Screwdriver
Carpenter's level
Wallboard tools

 MATERIALS

Plywood ($\frac{1}{8}$", $\frac{3}{4}$")
1 x 2 lumber
Wood glue

Flooring screws (2" No. 8)
Wood screws (3" No. 10)
Angle irons
Wallboard patching
   materials

 **SAFETY TIPS**

When using a power tool, protect your eyes with goggles.

DESKTOP SHELVING

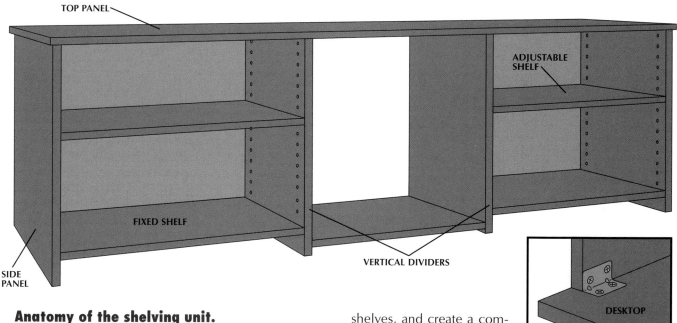

TOP PANEL

ADJUSTABLE SHELF

FIXED SHELF

VERTICAL DIVIDERS

SIDE PANEL

DESKTOP

Anatomy of the shelving unit.

Three fixed bottom shelves run between two side panels and vertical dividers, with the middle shelf positioned below the other two to allow the fastening of all these shelves to the dividers. The side panels are joined by a top panel that overlaps them at the front and sides. Two vertical dividers help support the top and the bottom shelves, and create a compartment for a computer monitor. Adjustable shelves on either side provide for storage, and a hardboard back on each side section adds rigidity to the structure. The sides of the unit are anchored to the desktop with small angle irons *(inset)*.

CONSTRUCTING A WALL UNIT

Assembling and hanging the unit.

◆ From $\frac{3}{4}$-inch plywood, cut the top, the bottom, the fixed shelf, and the sides (page 95, Step 1). Cut a plywood back panel to fit in the frame formed by other pieces.

◆ Cut matching dadoes $\frac{1}{8}$ inch wide and $\frac{1}{4}$ inch deep at the desired intervals across the top of the fixed shelf and the underside of the top to accommodate the dividers. Finish exposed edges (page 88).

◆ Clamp the pieces together and drill pilot holes for 2-inch No. 8 counterbored flooring screws, then fasten the panels together with glue and screws.

◆ With a carpenter's level, mark a level line on the wall for the bottom of the cabinet. Cut a 1-by-2 ledger the length of the cabinet and, with 3-inch No. 10 wood screws, fasten it to the studs so its top is even with the line.

◆ Have a helper hold the unit on the ledger.

◆ Near the top and middle of the unit, and every 12 inches in between, drill pilot holes for 3-inch No. 10 wood screws through the back into each stud (right). Screw the unit to the wall.

◆ Cut $\frac{1}{8}$-inch plywood divider panels to fit in the dadoes and slide them into place (inset).

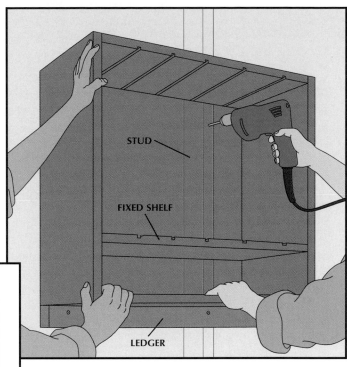

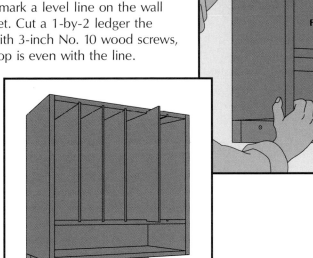

MOUNTING RECESSED SHELVES

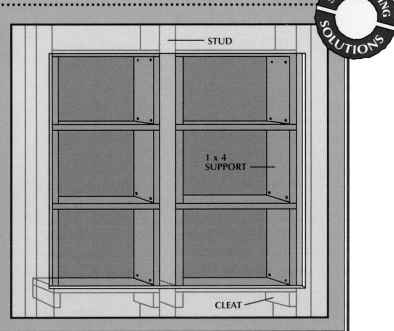

You can fit shelves in an opening made by cutting away wallboard between studs. Built from 1-by-4s, the shelves rest flush with the studs' edges. The bottom shelves rest on 1-by-2 cleats fastened to stud faces. Lengths of 1-by-4 attached to the studs support the middle shelves. At the top of each unit, a board the same size as the shelves is nailed to two 1-by-4 supports to form an inverted U; the assembly is inserted into the top of the wall opening and nailed to the studs. The perimeter of the opening can be smoothed with spackling compound or adhesive joint tape and framed with molding for a more finished look.

Consider tucking a small office into a closet; if the space is not deep enough to accommodate a computer, it can still be used for desk work. To adapt a closet, you may need to widen the opening and install bifold doors *(pages 43-45)* or a pair of prehung doors. Then, install storage shelves and a work surface *(below)*. Pages 86 to 93 explain how to prepare and join the wood.

Hanging Shelves: The sturdiest and most versatile shelves are ones supported by a system of standards and brackets. To support heavy items, mount heavy-duty brackets with a pair of prongs that snap into the standard, rather than just a single prong; and choose a system where the shelves fasten to the brackets rather than just rest on them *(opposite)*. To anchor the

shelving system solidly, fasten each standard to a wall stud. For shelves, choose material that can span the 16 inches between studs without sagging *(page 86)*. Locate the bottom shelf high enough to clear any equipment you plan to install on the work surface below.

The Work Surface: If the closet is deep enough, put in a desk. If it is not, consider hanging a work surface from cleats fastened to the closet wall *(pages 120-121)*, positioning it at a comfortable height *(page 81)*.

Recovering Hidden Space: To expand a closet office, you can store a rolling cabinet under the work surface *(page 109)*, and mount light-duty shelves on the end walls or to the backs of prehung doors *(page 121)*.

TOOLS

Electronic stud finder	Screwdriver
	Carpenter's level
Electric drill	Circular saw
Countersink bit	C-clamps

MATERIALS

Heavy-duty shelf standards and brackets	1 x 3s
	Wood screws
Plywood ($\frac{3}{4}$")	($1\frac{1}{4}$", 2" No. 8;
1 x 2s	3" No. 10)
	Wood glue

SAFETY TIPS

Put on goggles when you are using a power saw or drill.

Anatomy of a converted closet.
This closet holds a work surface supported by cleats fastened to the back and end walls. The front edge of the work surface is reinforced with an apron that interlocks with the end cleats. Enough space has been left between the front edge of the work surface and the doors for a desk chair to remain in the office when the doors are closed. A group of five standards supports two sets of shelves on brackets, which are staggered to share the center standard.

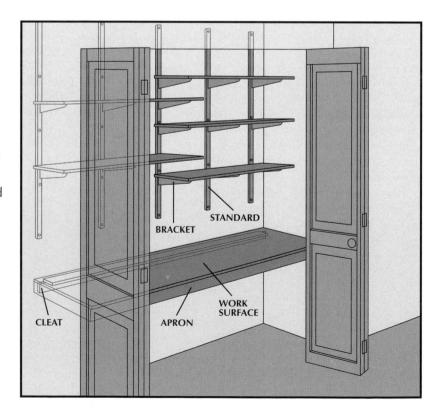

HANGING THE SHELVES

1. Attaching the first standard.

◆ Locate the studs at the back of the closet with a stud finder and mark the drywall at the middle of each stud with a vertical line.

◆ Hold the first standard in position centered over a line and mark the top screwhole.

◆ Remove the standard and drill a pilot hole for one of the screws provided.

◆ Replace the standard and drive the screw almost all the way *(right)*.

◆ Allow the standard to hang plumb, then mark the remaining screw holes.

◆ Swing the standard sideways to drill pilot holes, then drive the rest of the screws.

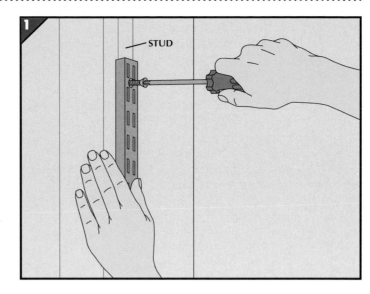

2. Fastening the remaining uprights.

◆ Insert a shelf bracket in the first standard, and another in the same position on a second standard.

◆ Place the second standard against the wall over a stud and set a level across the brackets. Adjust the height of the second standard so the brackets are level, then mark the top of the second standard on the wall *(left)*.

◆ Install the second standard as you did the first, ensuring that its top edge is in line with the mark.

◆ Repeat this procedure to install the rest of the standards.

◆ Snap the brackets into the standards at the desired height, then cut shelves at least 2 inches longer than the distance between the end brackets, finish exposed edges *(page 88)*, and mount the shelves.

◆ Fasten the shelves to the brackets with the screws provided, the longer screws in the back and the shorter ones in the front *(inset)*.

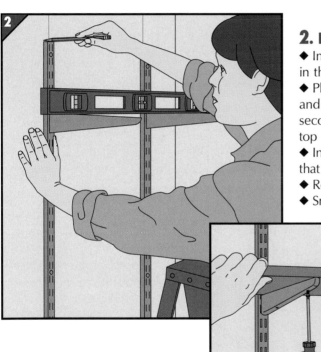

TRICKS OF THE TRADE

Supporting the Ends of Shelves

If your standard-and-bracket system does not call for fastening the shelves to the brackets, you will need to cut the shelves to overlap the brackets by a couple of inches. Doing so may be difficult if the last bracket is close to the end of the closet. To prevent the shelf from slipping off, screw two small metal plates to the end of each shelf *(right)* and hook the plates over the outside of the brackets.

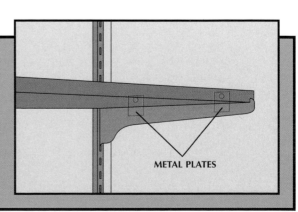

METAL PLATES

INSTALLING THE WORK SURFACE

1. Preparing the cleats.

◆ For the back cleat, cut one 1-by-3 to the length of the closet and another 5 inches shorter.
◆ With C-clamps, secure the two boards to the edge of a worktable *(right)* with $2\frac{1}{2}$ inches of the longer board extending at each end. Starting 1 inch from the end, drill pilot holes for 2-inch No. 8 countersunk wood screws every 12 inches through the shorter piece into the longer one.
◆ Fasten the pieces together with glue and screws.
◆ For each 1-by-3 end cleat, cut one piece $1\frac{3}{4}$ inches shorter than the depth of the work surface and a second piece $\frac{3}{4}$ inch shorter than the first.
◆ Fasten the end cleats together with glue and screws spaced at 12-inch intervals so the longer piece extends $\frac{3}{4}$ inch past the lower one to interlock with the back cleat *(inset).*

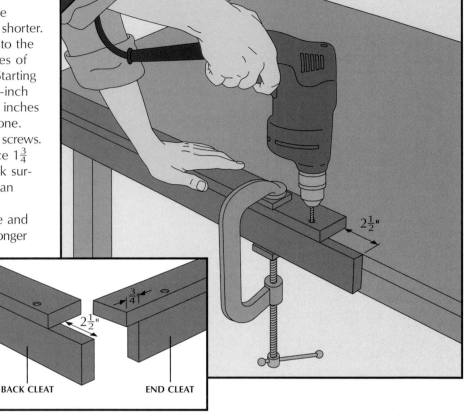

BACK CLEAT

END CLEAT

2. Mounting the cleats.

◆ Mark the back wall of the closet $\frac{3}{4}$ inch below the desired height of the work surface.
◆ With a helper, hold the back cleat against the wall with its top edge at the mark and level it.
◆ Drill a pilot hole for a 3-inch No. 10 wood screw through the cleat and into a stud near each end of the cleat *(left),* and drive the screws. Then drive a screw into each remaining stud.
◆ Interlock an end cleat with one corner of the back cleat *(inset),* and fasten it to the wall. Fasten the other end cleat in the same way.

BACK CLEAT

END CLEAT

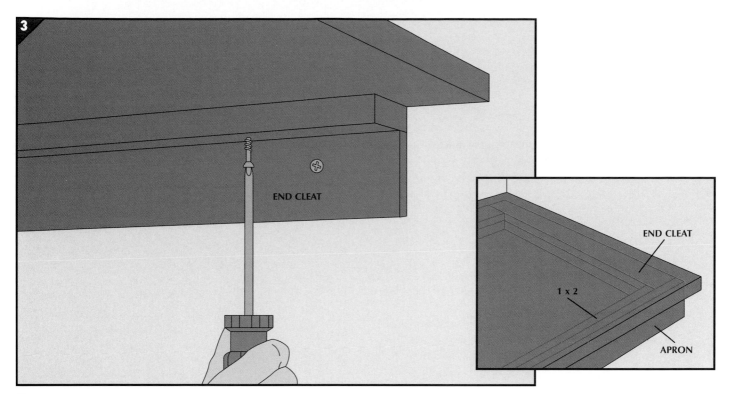

END CLEAT

END CLEAT

1 x 2

APRON

3. Adding the work surface.

◆ Cut the work surface and, after finishing the exposed edge *(page 88)*, set it on the cleats.

◆ With a helper holding the work surface down, drill pilot holes for $1\frac{1}{4}$-inch No. 8 wood screws up through the projecting part of the cleats into the work surface, locating the holes every 12 inches.

◆ Drive the screws *(above)*.

◆ For the apron that will support the work surface's front edge, cut a 1-by-3 to the length of the closet and a 1-by-2 that is 5 inches shorter.

◆ Position the 1-by-2 against the 1-by-3 face to face with their top edges flush so the 1-by-3 extends $2\frac{1}{2}$ inches past each end of the 1-by-2. Drill pilot holes for 2-inch No. 8 wood screws every 12 inches through the 1-by-2

into the 1-by-3 and glue and screw them together.

◆ Fit the apron into place, interlocking it with the end cleats *(inset)*; clamp it to the top.

◆ Drill pilot holes for 2-inch screws up through the apron's 1-by-2 and into the underside of the work surface, spacing the holes every 12 inches. Glue and screw the apron in place.

HIDDEN SPACE BEHIND A DOOR

The back of a prehung closet door can offer useful storage space. A wire shelf unit *(right)* can keep small office supplies at hand when the door is open; other types are available to hold large items, such as file folders. To make sure the door can close, buy shelves no deeper than the space between the front edge of the work surface and the front of the closet. Alternatively, hang the shelves high enough so they will clear the work surface when the door is closed. To hang the shelves, use hollow-wall anchors with short shanks specially designed for hollow-core doors.

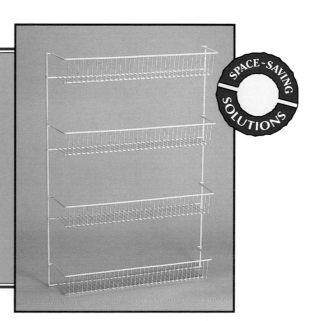

SPACE-SAVING SOLUTIONS

When lack of space for a home office is a problem, consider building a work surface that folds against the wall. You can install such a desk in a small office, or even in an area such as the living room that is doing double duty as an office. The desk is stored out of the way against the wall, ready to be set up when needed.

Designing the Desk: Plan to install the desk at a comfortable height for working *(page 81)*. Although you can design it with a depth and length that best suits your needs, there are a couple of constraints: For the legs to fold back against the desktop, the top must be longer than the legs; and for the desk to rest flat against the wall, it must be higher than it is deep.

TOOLS

Circular saw
Electric drill
Countersink bit
Screwdriver
Table saw
Dado blade
Hacksaw
Carpenter's level
Electronic stud
  finder

MATERIALS

Plywood ($\frac{3}{4}$")
2 x 2s, 2 x 4s
Flooring screws
  ($1\frac{1}{4}$", 2" No. 8)
Wood screws
  ($\frac{5}{8}$" No. 6; 4" No. 10)
Piano hinges
Locking braces
Wood glue

 SAFETY TIPS

When using power tools, protect your eyes with goggles.

Anatomy of a folding desk.
The work surface is hinged to a 2-by-4 ledger fastened to the wall. An apron of 2-by-2s frames three sides of the desktop, lending it rigidity. When the desk is open, its front edge is supported by a pair of 2-by-4 legs. Each leg has a plywood plate set into it which is hinged to the bottom of the desktop; locking braces hold the legs open. Adjustable feet *(page 97)* help level the desktop.

To store the desk, the locking braces are released and the legs are folded up against the top *(inset)*; the table is then lowered against the wall. The apron hides the ends of the folded legs.

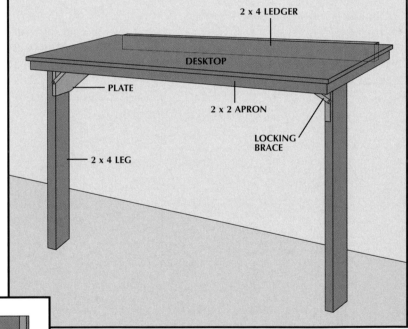

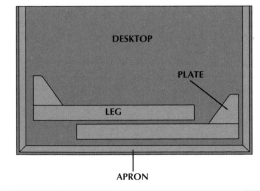

ASSEMBLING THE DESK

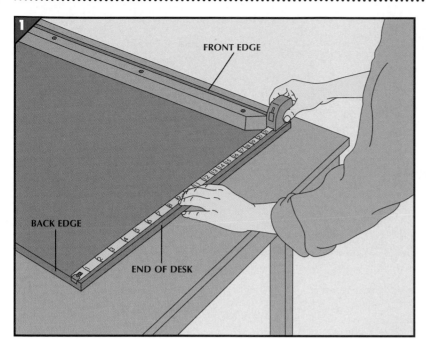

FRONT EDGE

BACK EDGE

END OF DESK

1. Attaching the apron to the top.

◆ From $\frac{3}{4}$-inch plywood, cut the desktop to the desired size and set it face down on a work surface.
◆ Cut a 2-by-2 apron piece 2 inches shorter than the top, and miter both ends to a 45-degree angle. Position the piece parallel to and 1 inch from the front edge of the top, centering it between the ends of the top.
◆ Drill pilot holes for countersunk 2-inch No. 8 flooring screws, spaced every 12 inches, and fasten the 2-by-2 to the top with glue and screws.
◆ Measure from one outside edge of the apron piece to the back edge of the top (left), and cut two 2-by-2s to this length, mitering one end of each board.
◆ Fasten the 2-by-2s to the top in the same way as the first 2-by-2, parallel to and 1 inch from the edges, so the mitered ends meet those of the first 2-by-2.

2. Assembling the legs.

◆ Cut 2-by-4 legs to the desired height.
◆ With a router or a table saw and dado blade, cut a rabbet at one end of each leg $\frac{3}{4}$ inch deep and 6 inches wide.
◆ From $\frac{3}{4}$-inch plywood, cut two plates 10 inches long and 6 inches wide, tapering an edge of each piece 4 inches from one end (inset).
◆ Fit a plate into the rabbet at the end of one leg. Drill four pilot holes for $1\frac{1}{4}$-inch No. 8 countersunk flooring screws and fasten the plate to the leg with glue and screws (right).
◆ With a hacksaw, cut a piano hinge to a length of 10 inches. Fasten one leaf of the hinge to the plate with $\frac{5}{8}$-inch No. 6 wood screws.

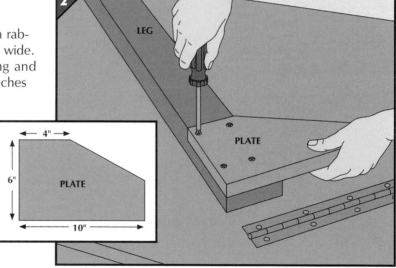

LEG

PLATE

4"

6"

PLATE

10"

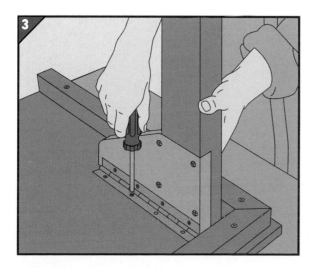

3. Attaching the legs to the top.

◆ Stand a leg in one of the corners formed by the front and side apron pieces, leaving $\frac{1}{2}$ inch between the leg and the front apron board for the locking braces you will install.
◆ Fasten the free leaf of the piano hinge to the top with $\frac{5}{8}$-inch No. 6 wood screws (left).
◆ Fold the leg down against the desktop.
◆ Position the second leg so it will clear the first when folded (inset, opposite), and fasten it to the desktop.

4. Bracing the legs.

◆ Open one of the locking braces all the way and position it against the leg and the top so the distances indicated as A and B in the illustration are equal.

◆ Fasten the brace to the leg and top with the screws provided, driving the screws only partway *(right)*.

◆ Check that the leg folds properly. Adjust the location of the brace if necessary and drive the screws the rest of the way.

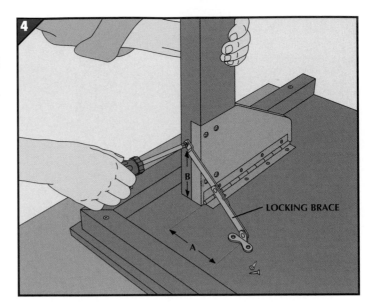

5. Attaching the hinge to the top.

◆ Cut a length of piano hinge to fit between the side apron pieces attached to the top.

◆ Fasten the hinge to the underside of the top, flush with the back edge, driving $\frac{5}{8}$-inch No. 6 wood screws into each end hole and every second hole in between.

6. Mounting the desk.

◆ Mark a level line on the wall at the height of the top surface of the desk. Locate and mark the studs along the line.

◆ Cut a 2-by-4 ledger to fit between the apron pieces fastened to the top. Have a helper hold the ledger with its top edge even with the line on the wall and check it for level. Then, drill pilot holes for 4-inch No. 10 countersunk wood screws through the ledger and into each stud, and fasten the ledger to the wall.

◆ Make two temporary legs by cutting two 2-by-4s to the same length as the permanent legs.

◆ Lock the permanent legs in the open position and set the desk upright with its back edge against the face of the ledger and its top surface flush with the top edge of the ledger. Prop up the back of the desk with the temporary legs.

◆ From under the desk, fasten the free leaf of the piano hinge to the ledger with $\frac{5}{8}$-inch No. 6 wood screws driven through every second screw hole *(right)*.

◆ Remove the temporary legs.

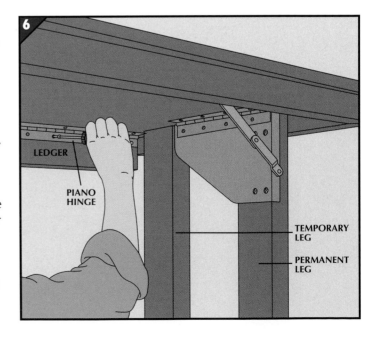

Furniture made of veneered MDF or good-quality plywood can be finished in the same way as solid-wood furniture. You can stain the wood, then apply a clear finish. On lower-quality plywood, fill surface defects and use paint.

Preparing the Surface: Before finishing your furniture, sand its surfaces. Using a belt or orbital sander, or working by hand, start with 120-grit sandpaper and follow with 220-grit. Remove sanding dust with a tack rag. After sanding, repair cracks or gouges in the surface with wood filler. Even minor blemishes will show through a clear finish.

Staining: Penetrating stains soak into the wood and color the fibers, accentuating the grain. The nonpenetrating variety covers the wood with a colored film and fills the wood pores, obscuring the grain. This type is a good choice for coarse-grained woods.

Stains are made with various solvents as the base, including water, oil, and alcohol. Oil-base stains are the easiest to work with; they are simply wiped on with a sponge or cheesecloth.

Before applying a stain, coat wood plugs and any other exposed end grain with sealer; use shellac for water- or oil-base stains and oil-base wood conditioner for alcohol-base products.

Applying a Clear Finish: Polyurethane varnish is ideal for surfaces that must stand up to wear because it dries to a clear, high-gloss surface that is durable and resistant to spills. This type of varnish is applied with a brush in several coats *(below)*; the more coats applied, the more lustrous the finish.

 MATERIALS

Sandpaper
  (220-, 400-grit)
Tack rag
Varnish

 **SAFETY TIPS**

When applying varnish, put on goggles and nitrile gloves.

Brushing on polyurethane varnish.
◆ Dilute the varnish as recommended by the manufacturer.
◆ Place the furniture on scrap-wood props.
◆ Dip a paintbrush into the varnish to half the length of the bristles and apply a heavy load of finish to a small area, working across the grain.
◆ Without reloading the brush, go back over the area, brushing with the grain *(right)*.
◆ To smooth the finish, lightly run the tip of a nearly dry brush over the area, holding the brush almost perpendicular to the surface and working with the grain. Cover the rest of the furniture in the same way.
◆ Let the finish dry as recommended on the label, then press your thumb against the surface and wipe the area with a soft cloth; if the thumbprint remains, more drying time is needed.
◆ With 220-grit sandpaper, rub the surface lightly and evenly, working with the grain. Remove the dust with a tack rag.
◆ Apply additional coats in the same way as the first, letting each one dry and sanding it before applying the next coat.

◆ Allow the final coat to dry for 24 hours, then if desired, polish the finish to a soft sheen with 400-grit sandpaper.

INDEX

TIME® LIFE BOOKS

Time-Life Books is a division of Time Life Inc.

TIME LIFE INC.
PRESIDENT and CEO: George Artandi

TIME-LIFE BOOKS
PRESIDENT: Stephen R. Frary
PUBLISHER/MANAGING EDITOR: Neil Kagan

HOME REPAIR AND IMPROVEMENT: Home Offices
EDITOR: Lee Hassig
MARKETING DIRECTOR: James Gillespie
Art Director: Kate McConnell
Associate Editor/Research and Writing: Karen Sweet
Marketing Manager: Wells Spence

Director of Finance: Christopher Hearing
Director of Book Production: Marjann Caldwell
Director of Operations: Betsi McGrath
Director of Photography and Research: John Conrad Weiser
Director of Editorial Administration: Barbara Levitt
Production Manager: Marlene Zack
Quality Assurance Manager: James King
Library: Louise D. Forstall

ST. REMY MULTIMEDIA INC.
President and Chief Executive Officer: Fernand Lecoq
President and Chief Operating Officer: Pierre Léveillé
Vice President, Finance: Natalie Watanabe
Managing Editor: Carolyn Jackson
Managing Art Director: Diane Denoncourt
Production Manager: Michelle Turbide

Staff for *Home Offices*

Series Editors: Marc Cassini, Heather Mills
Art Directors: Chantal Bilodeau, Michel Giguère
Assistant Editor: Rebecca Smollett
Designers: Jean-Guy Doiron, Robert Labelle
Editorial Assistants: Liane Keightley, James Piecowye
Coordinator: Dominique Gagné
Copy Editor: Judy Yelon
Indexer: Linda Cardella Cournoyer
Systems Coordinator: Edward Renaud
Technical Support: Jean Sirois
Other Staff: Éric Beaulieu, Hélène Dion, Lorraine Doré, Geneviève Dubé, Anne-Marie Lemay

PICTURE CREDITS
Cover: Photograph, Robert Chartier. Art, Maryo Proulx.

Illustrators: Jack Arthur, La Bande Créative, Frederic F. Bigio, Lazlo Bodrogi, Adolph E. Brotman, Roger C. Essley, Nicholas Fasciano, Charles Forsythe, William J. Hennessy Jr., Walter Hilmers Jr., Fred Holz, Dick Lee, Judy Lineberger, John Martinez, Peter McGinn, Joan S. McGurren, W. F. McWilliam, Jacques Perrault, Raymond Skibinski, Ian Sproull, Vantage Art, Inc., Vicki Vebell, Whitman Studio Inc.

Photographers: **End papers:** Glenn Moores and Chantal Lamarre. **39:** Renée Comet. **42:** Robert Chartier. **44:** Renée Comet. **49:** SL Waber Inc. **57:** Renée Comet. **62:** Glenn Moores and Chantal Lamarre. **73:** Robert Chartier. **75, 88, 89, 90, 99:** Glenn Moores and Chantal Lamarre. **103:** Sopa Inc. **108, 109, 111, 121:** Glenn Moores and Chantal Lamarre.

ACKNOWLEDGMENTS
The editors wish to thank the following individuals and institutions: Jon Arno, Troy, MI; Arrow Fastener Co., Saddle Brook, NJ; Balt Inc., Cameron, TX; Herman Miller Inc., Zeeland, MI; Home Tech Solutions, Cupertino, CA; Incotel Ltd., Montreal, Que; Paul McGoldrick, Pianoforte, Montreal, Que.; NCS, St. Laurent, Que.; Nutone Inc., Cincinnati, OH; Occupational Safety and Health Administration, Washington, DC; Peca Products, Jamesville, WI; Ira Shapiro, Architect, Redding, CT; SL Waber, Mount Laurel, NJ; Peter Smollett, Toronto, Ont.; Thomas & Betts, Rosemont, Que.; Thomas Lighting Accent Division, Los Angeles, CA; 3 Com, Skokie, IL; Tyfu Data Inc., Montreal, Que.; Woods Industries Inc, Camel, IN; The Woodworker's Store, Medina, MN

Library of Congress Cataloging-in-Publication Data
Home offices / by the editors of Time-Life Books.
p. cm. — (Home repair and improvement)
Includes index.
ISBN 0-7835-3914-2
1. Dwellings—Remodeling. 2. Home offices—Design and construction.
I. Time-Life Books. II. Series.
TH4816.3.O34H65   1997
643'.58—dc21   97-34434